The Forest Tower

The Danish Architectural Press
Camp Adventure
EFFEKT Architects

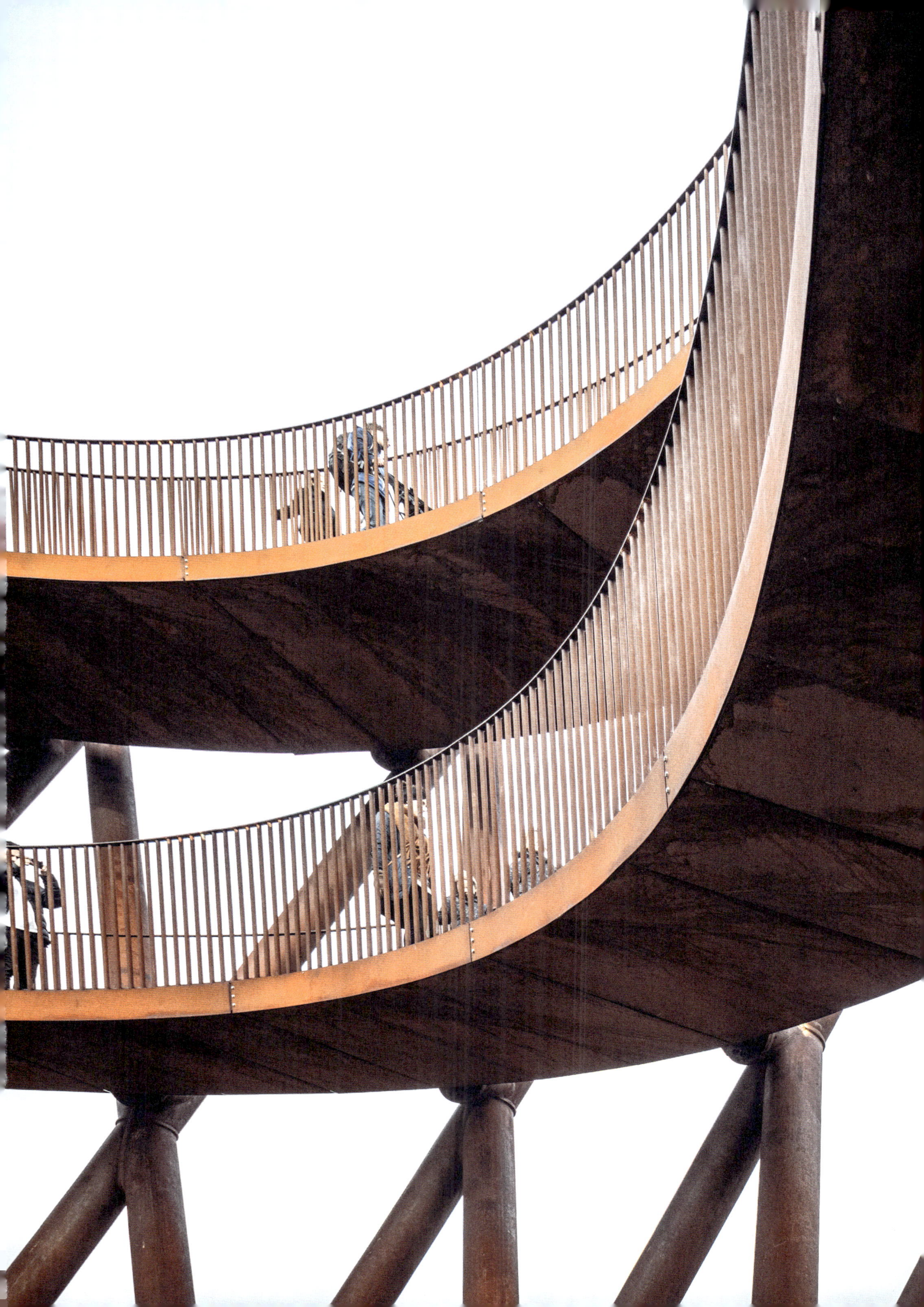

Contents

Foreword

On 31 March 2019, Camp Adventure opened Scandinavia's tallest observation tower, the Forest Tower. An architectural achievement inspired by nature, history and culture. More people should be able to enjoy nature. Nature should be used, protected, preserved and showcased as a setting for active nature experiences. From the outset, our vision was to offer a unique, extraordinary and unprecedented experience in a beautiful natural setting. And to attract international attention and visitors from all over the world. That vision has been fully accomplished.

The dream of creating Scandinavia's first big observation tower was realized within a very short time span. The project was even given permission to build in a protected forest on the lands of the beautiful and historical former monastery Gisselfeld Kloster – surrounded by precious and irreplaceable nature. From the outset, the mission was to bring people into nature to experience its beauty by showcasing it in new ways and making it more accessible. Always with respect for nature's inherent qualities and with a strong emphasis on aesthetics and quality.

We invested everything at our disposal in terms of economic and human resources, engaging in every stage of the process. With inspiration from around the world, we modified the original choice of materials, designed the route to and from the Forest Tower and held on to a clear vision of the kind of Forest Tower we wanted to create. From the decisions made at meetings or at a desk to the efforts of our own construction team – building boardwalks, installing planks on the Forest Tower ramp and building and then dismantling an entire interior tower – we have been engaged and committed throughout, meeting the deadlines we set and achieving our goal of creating a unique and outstanding attraction.

We chose to invest in top-quality architecture and sublime experiences, and we are thrilled that more than 350,000 visitors chose to visit the Forest Tower during the first year. A dedicated team of professional employees, builders and architects helped realize our dream of creating world-class experiences in the Danish landscape. We thank them all for their role in making it possible.

The future for Camp Adventure involves a wide range of initiatives, including a larger visitors' centre with meeting facilities, a restaurant and a shop, and we already offer unconventional accommodations for overnight stays. From the outset, Camp Adventure has had an international outlook, and we continue our effort to spread the concept to the rest of the world. The big international interest sparked by the Forest Tower makes it easier to share the good experiences and the closeness to nature with even more people – not just in Denmark. Media from Denmark and abroad have helped spread the story of the Forest Tower, which was included on *TIME Magazine*'s list of the World's 100 Greatest Places and has featured in anything from music videos to TV's annual Christmas advent calendar series and other TV shows. The outcome fully lives up to our hopes: the Forest Tower has become a destination for the many who wish to see and experience the nature of Denmark.

The book tells the story of the Forest Tower. It offers impressive in-depth photo documentation of a unique, privately funded project and a unique nature experience. Many thanks to the editor, graphic designers and photographer. The original idea for the publication came from Kasper Larsen. We wish you an enjoyable read.

—Jesper Mathiesen, founder of Camp Adventure

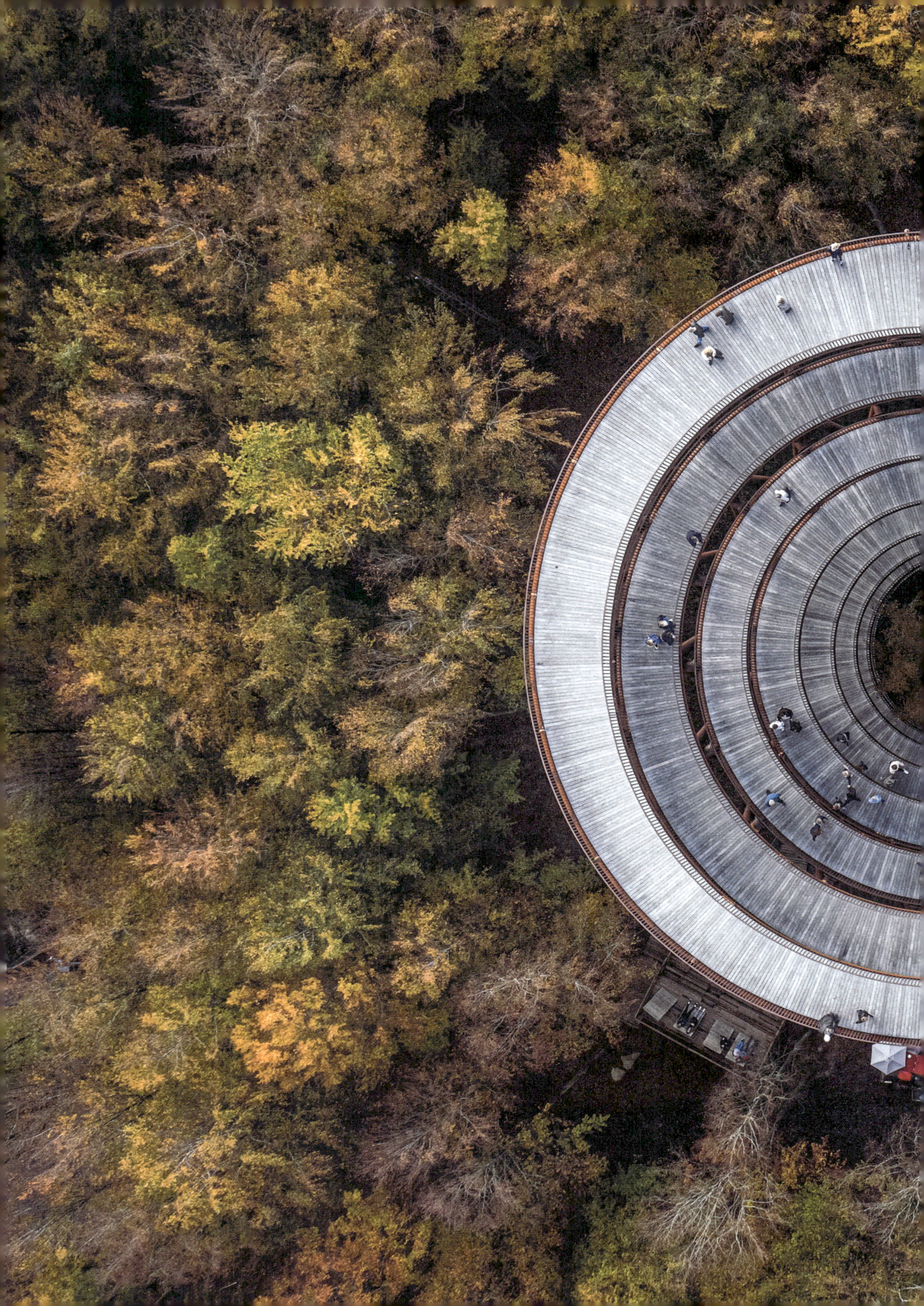

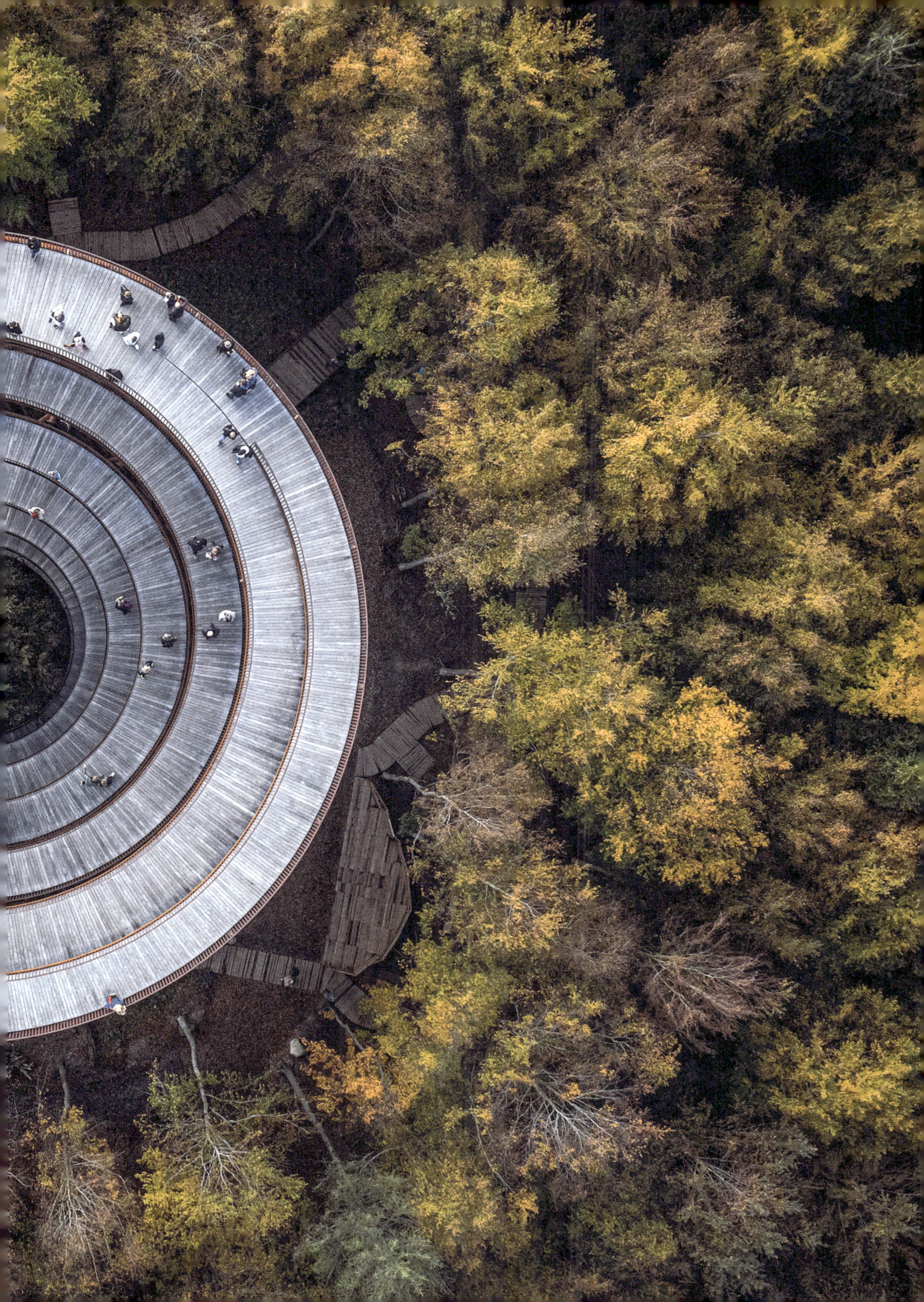

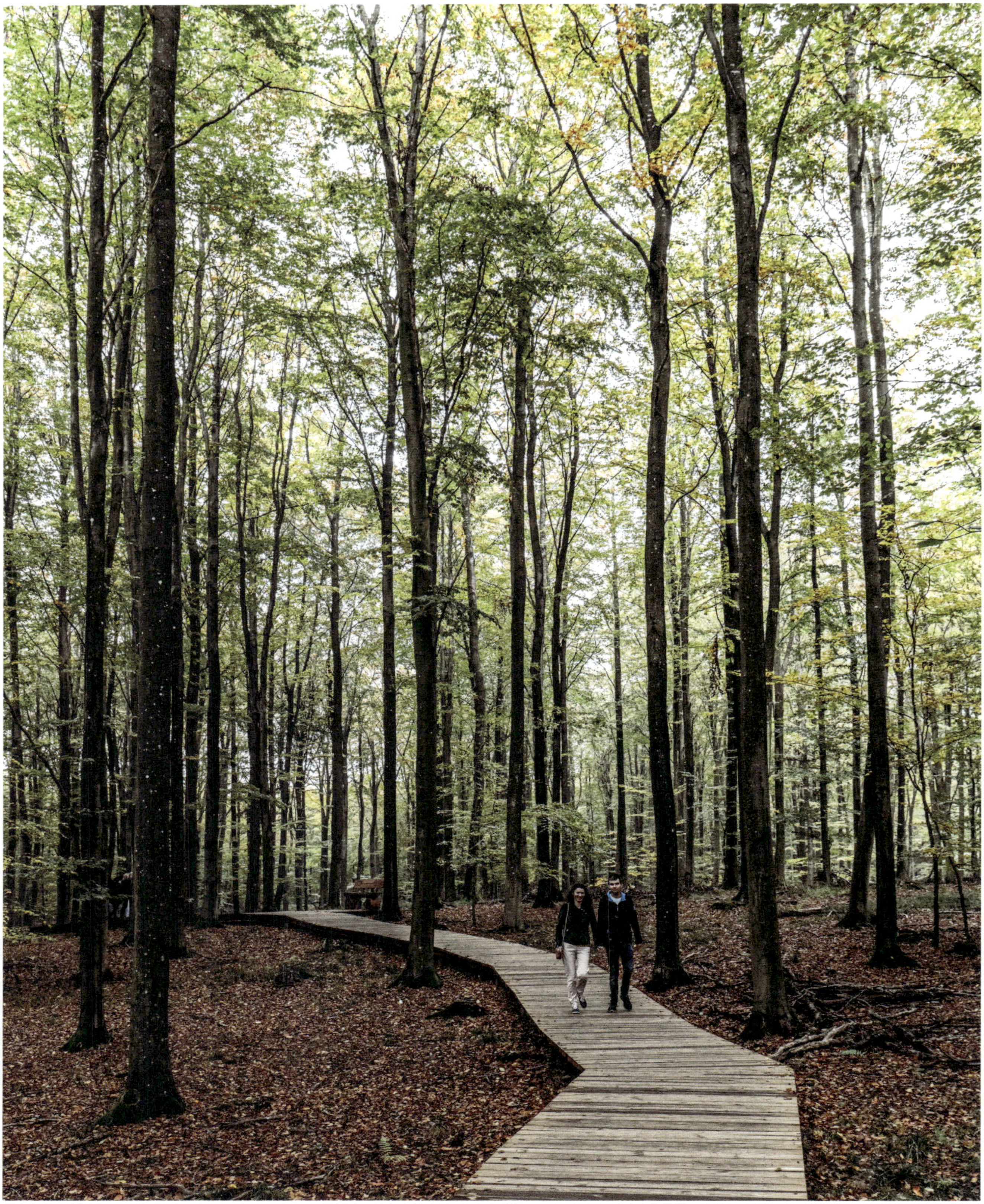

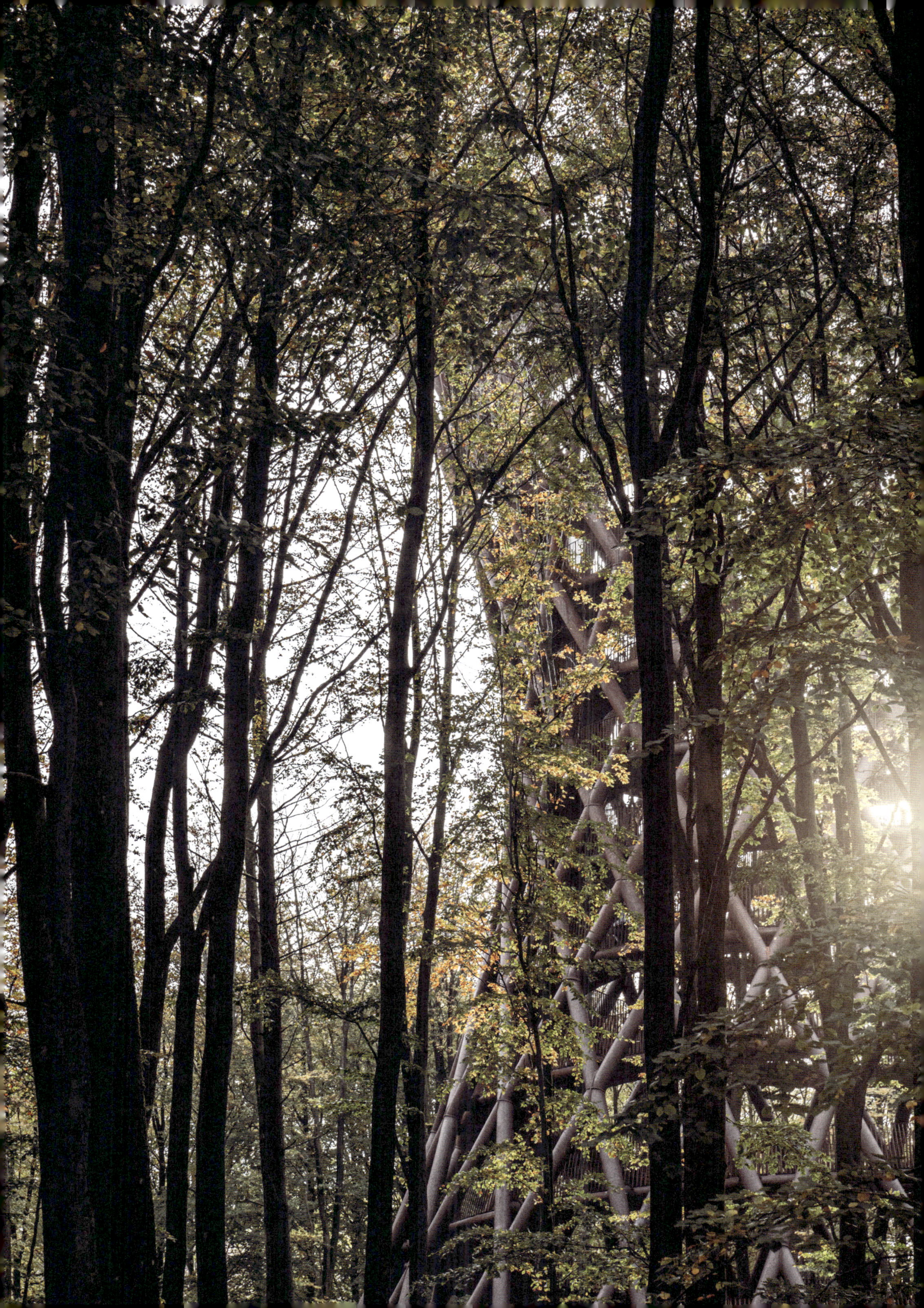

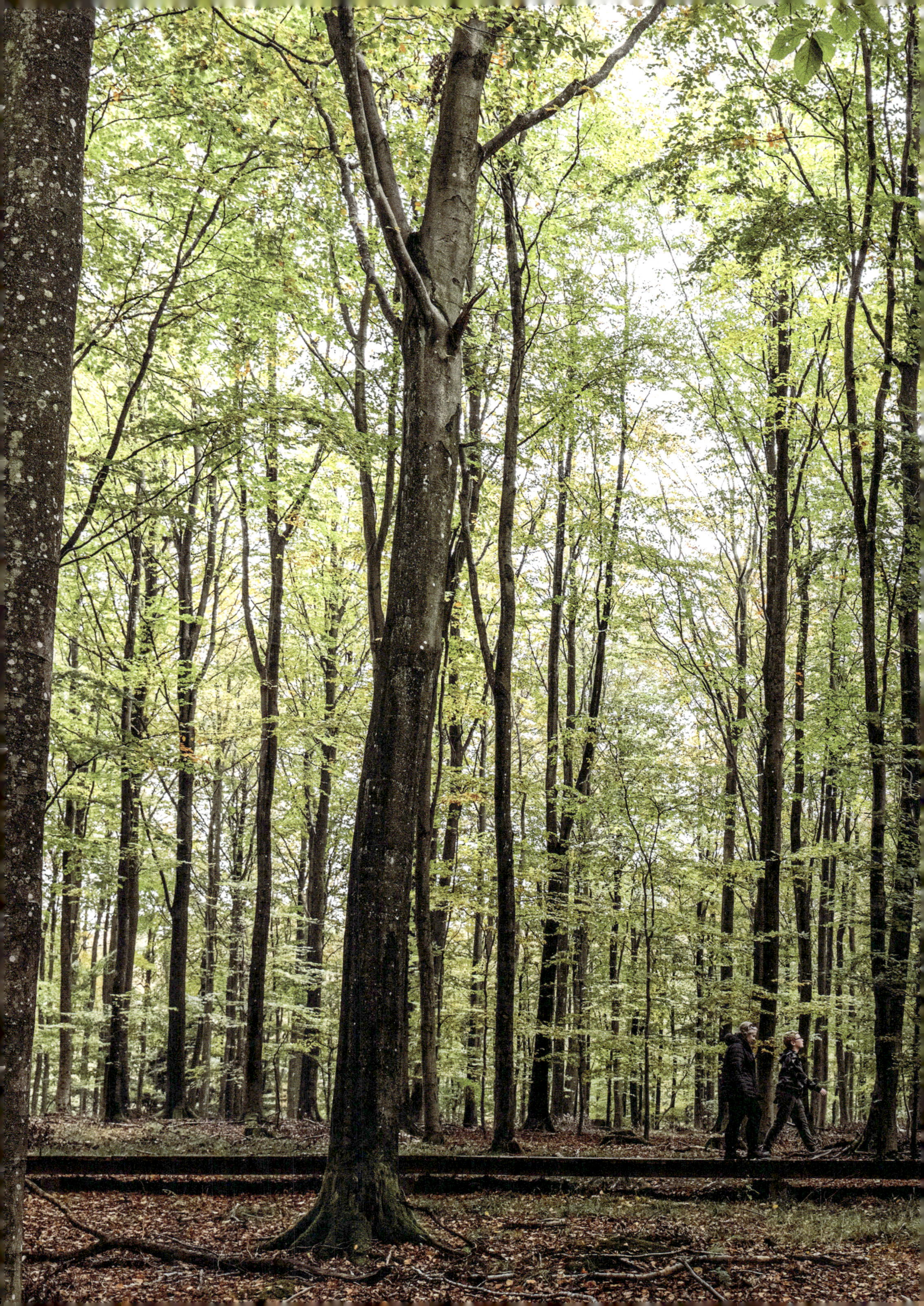

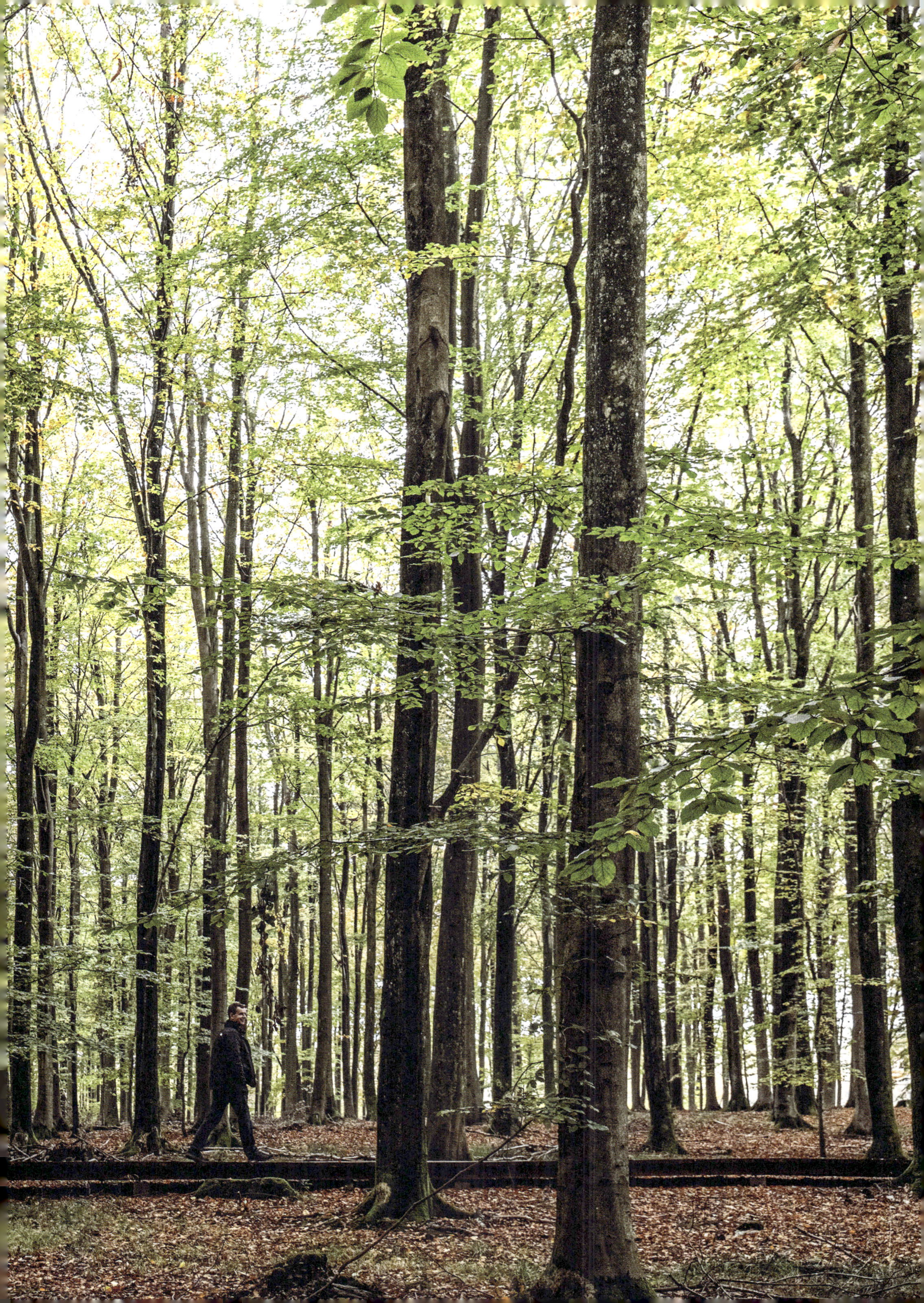

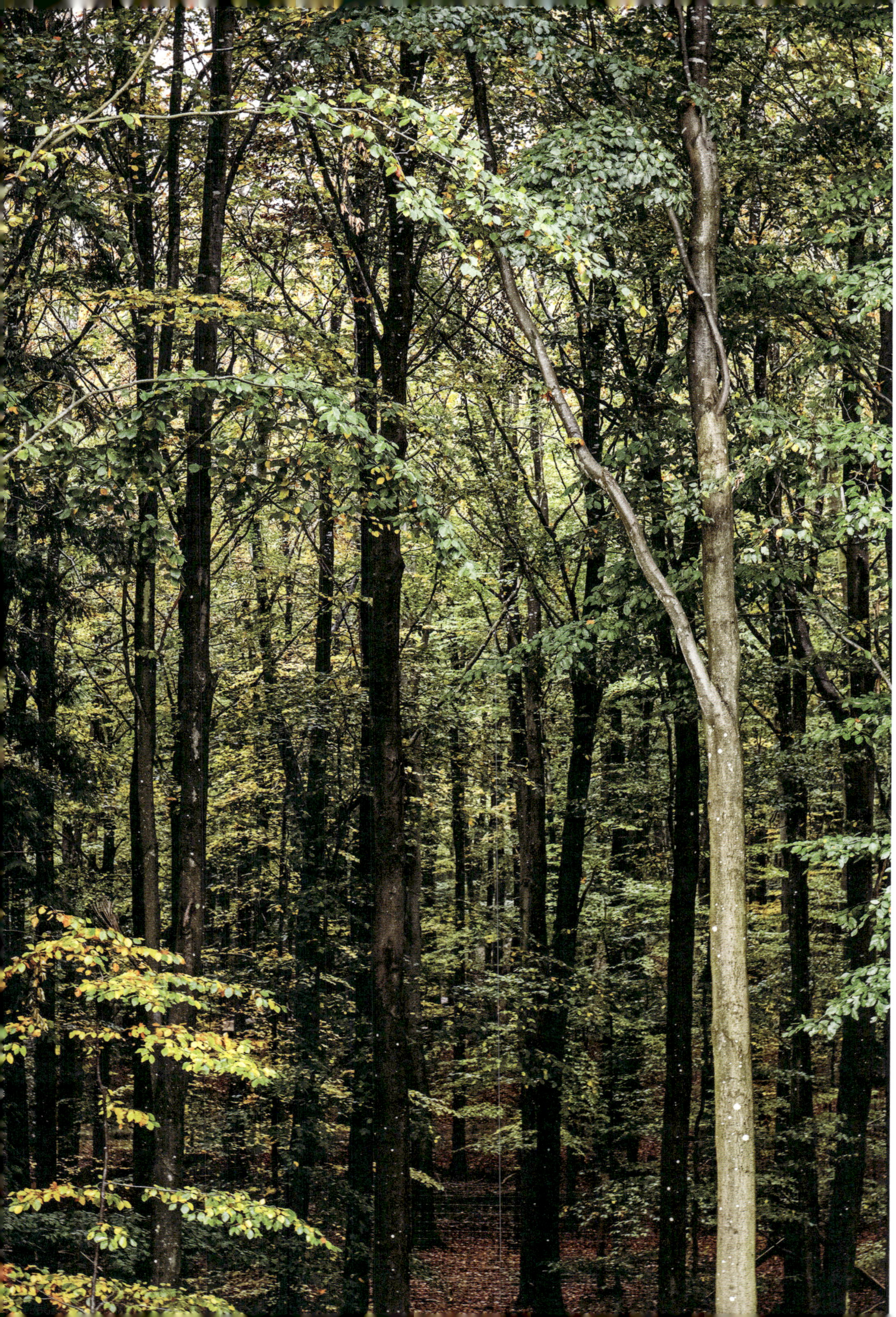

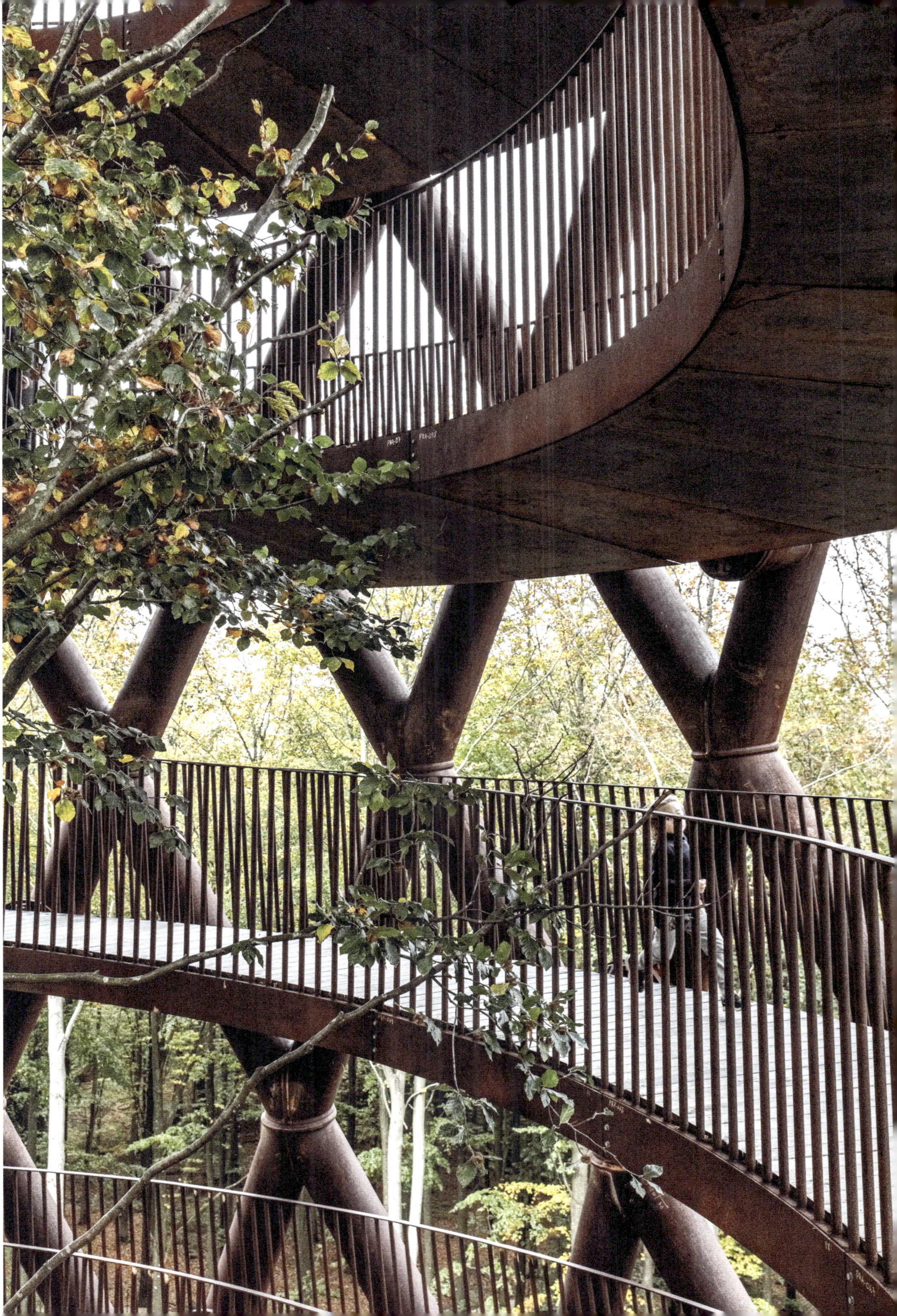

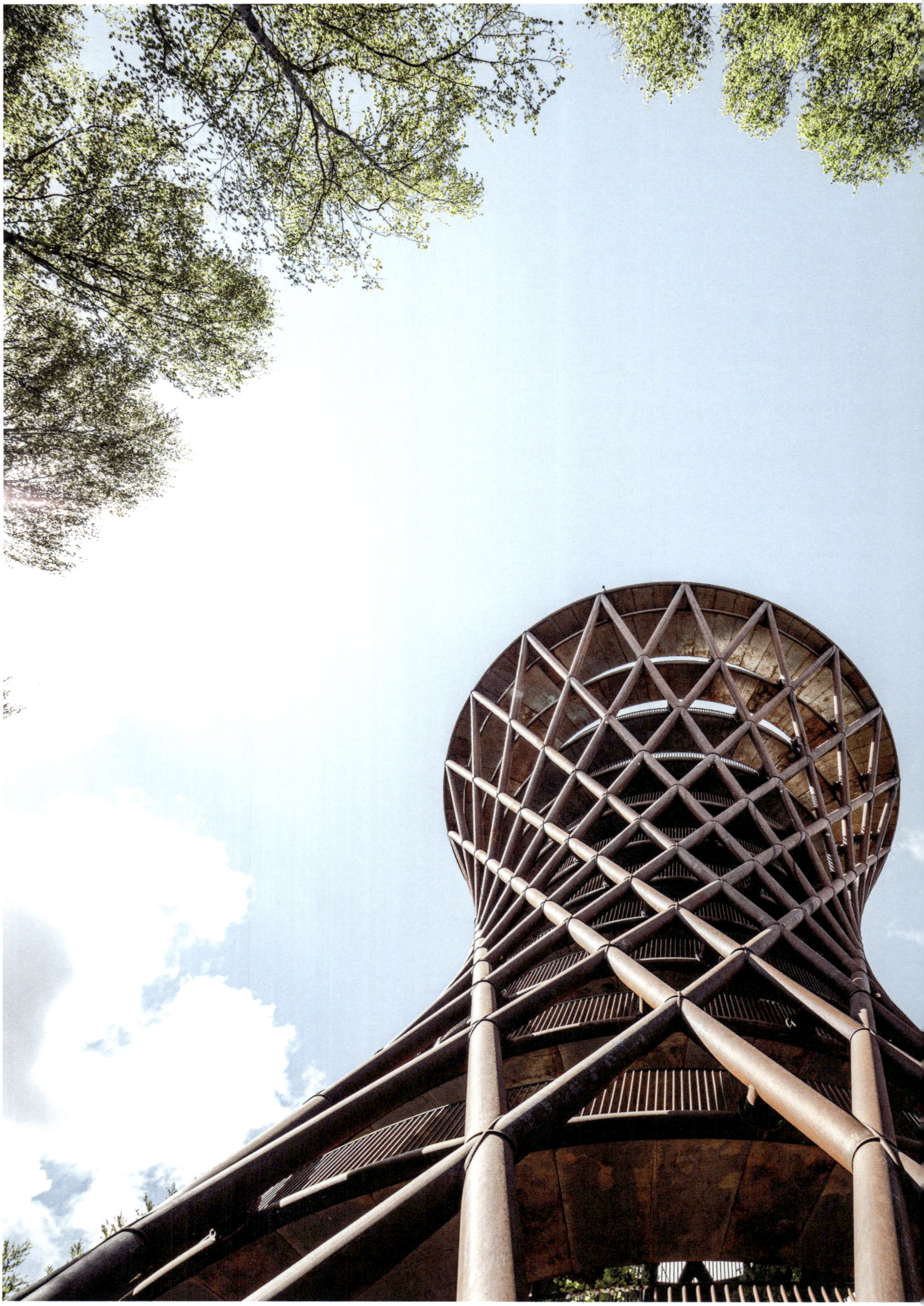

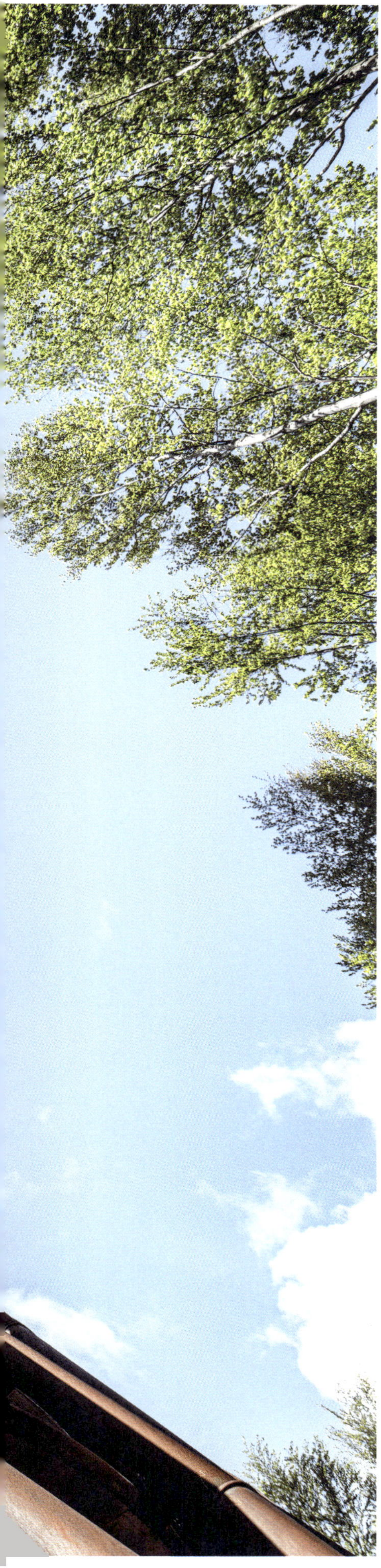

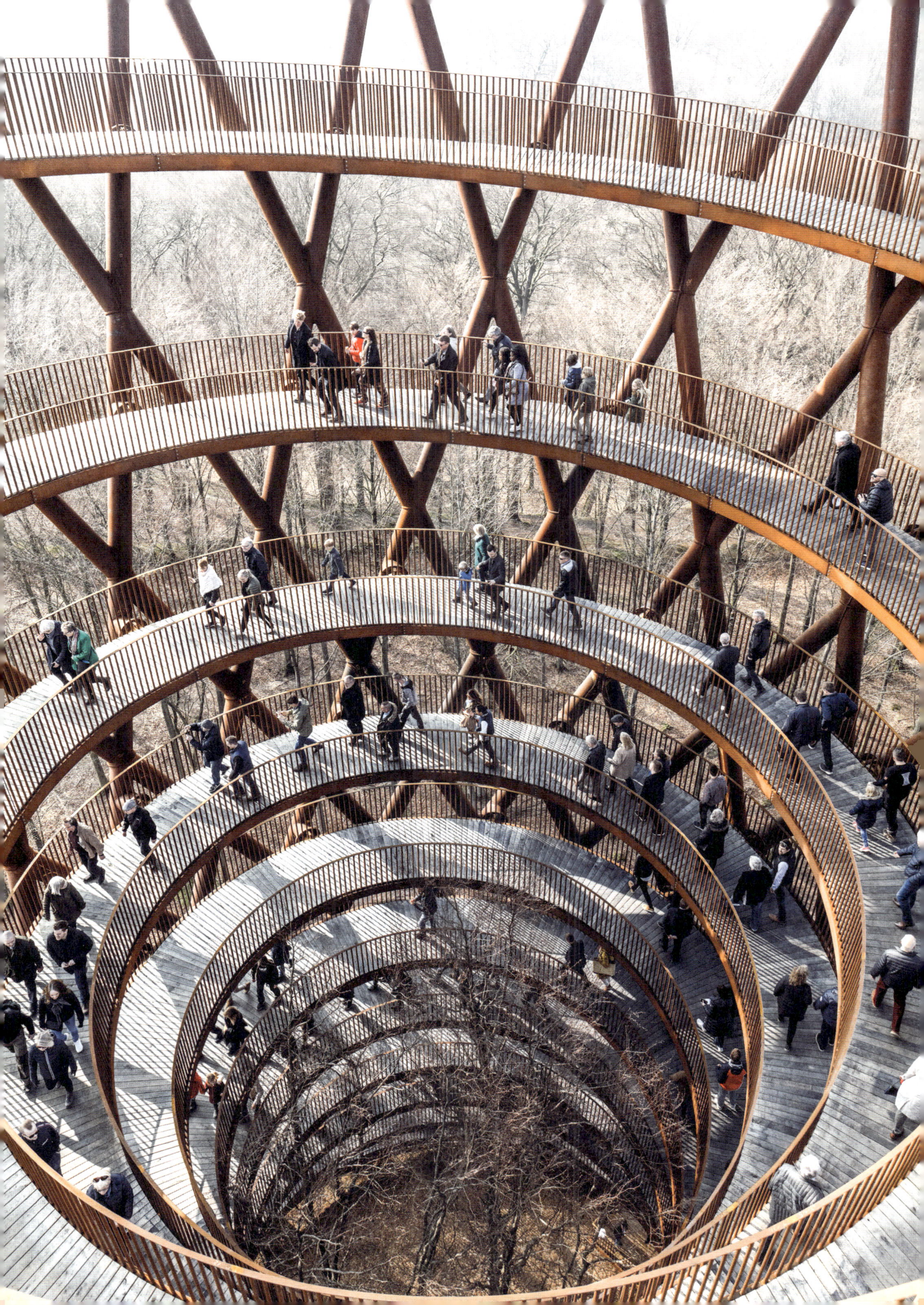

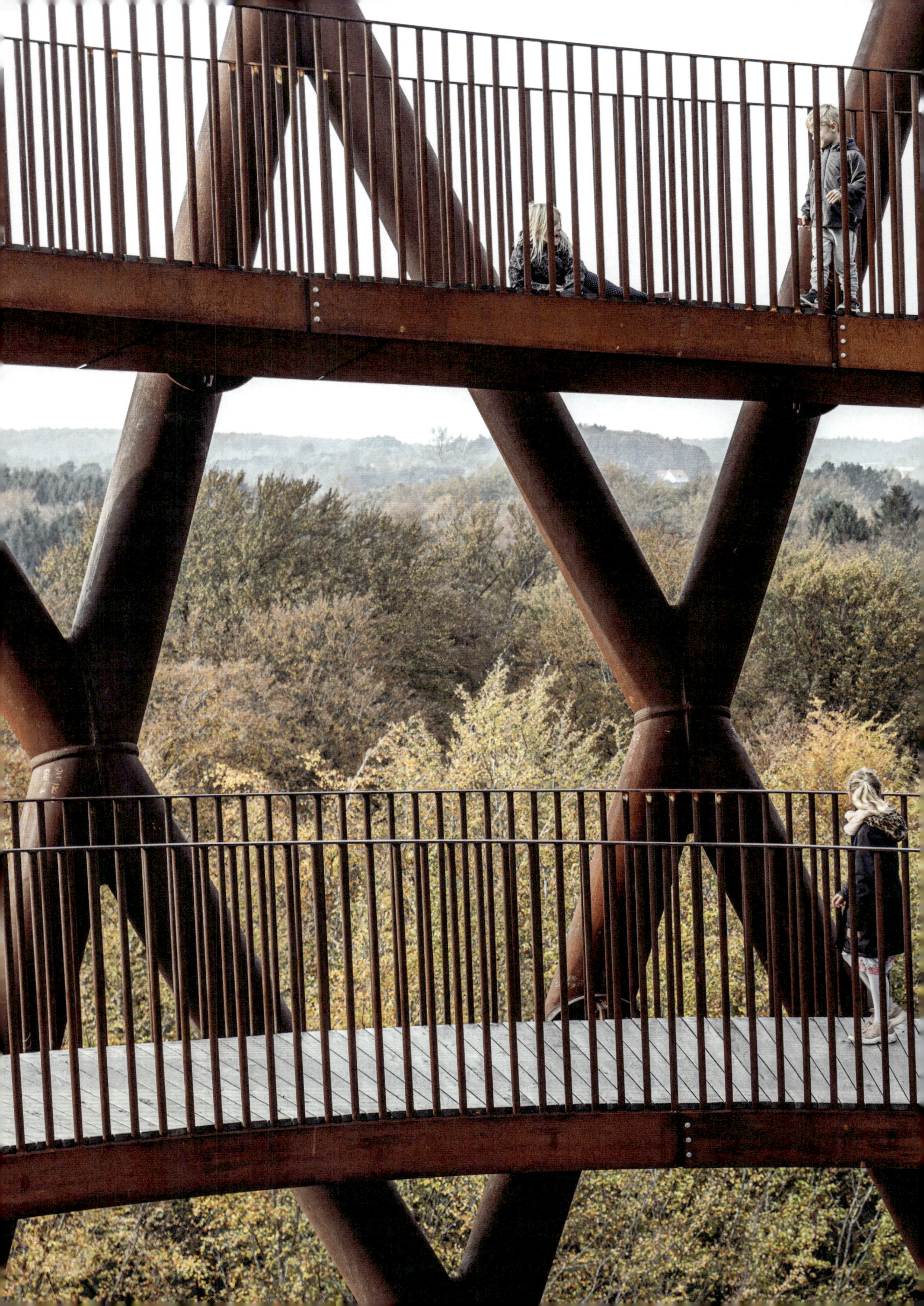

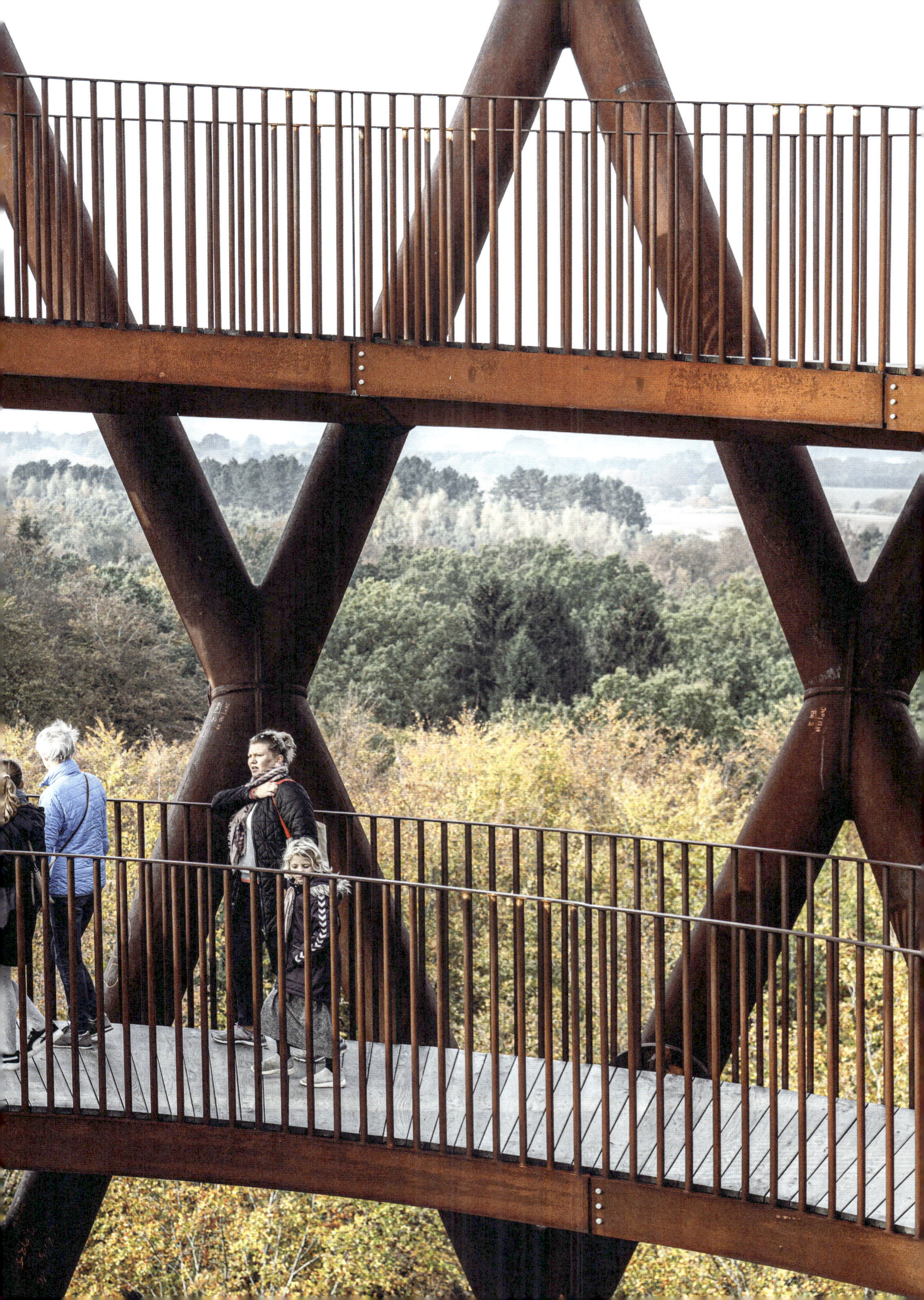

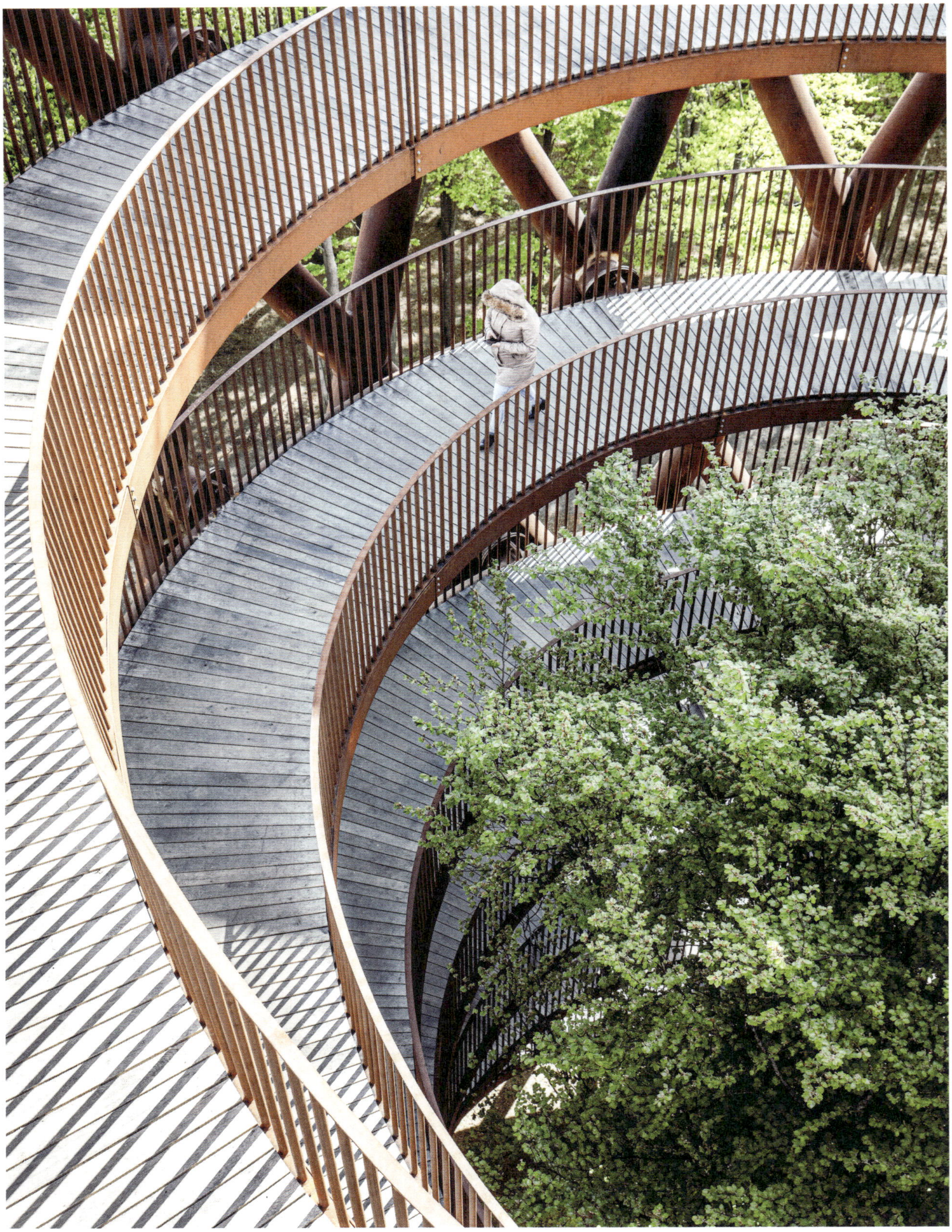

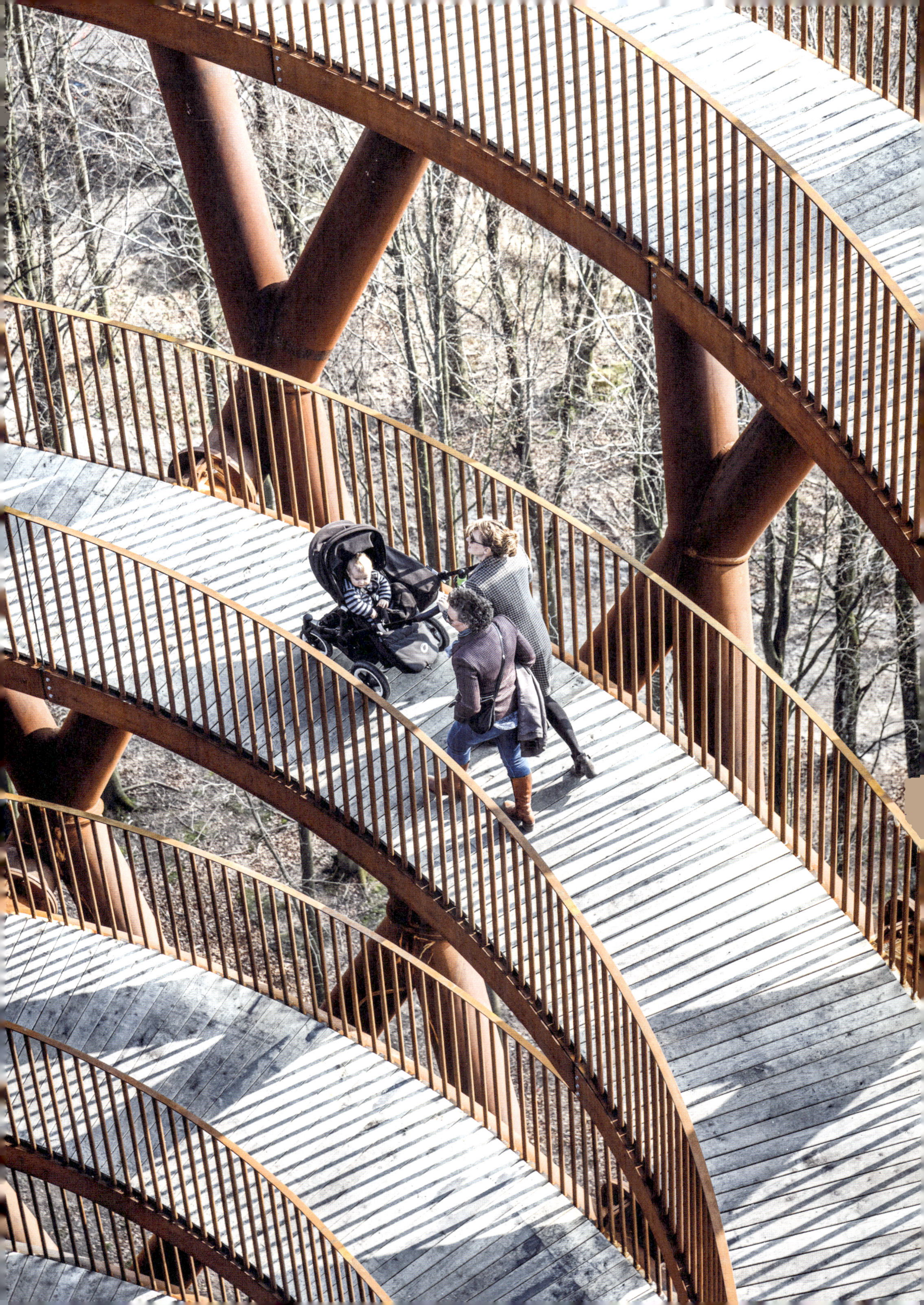

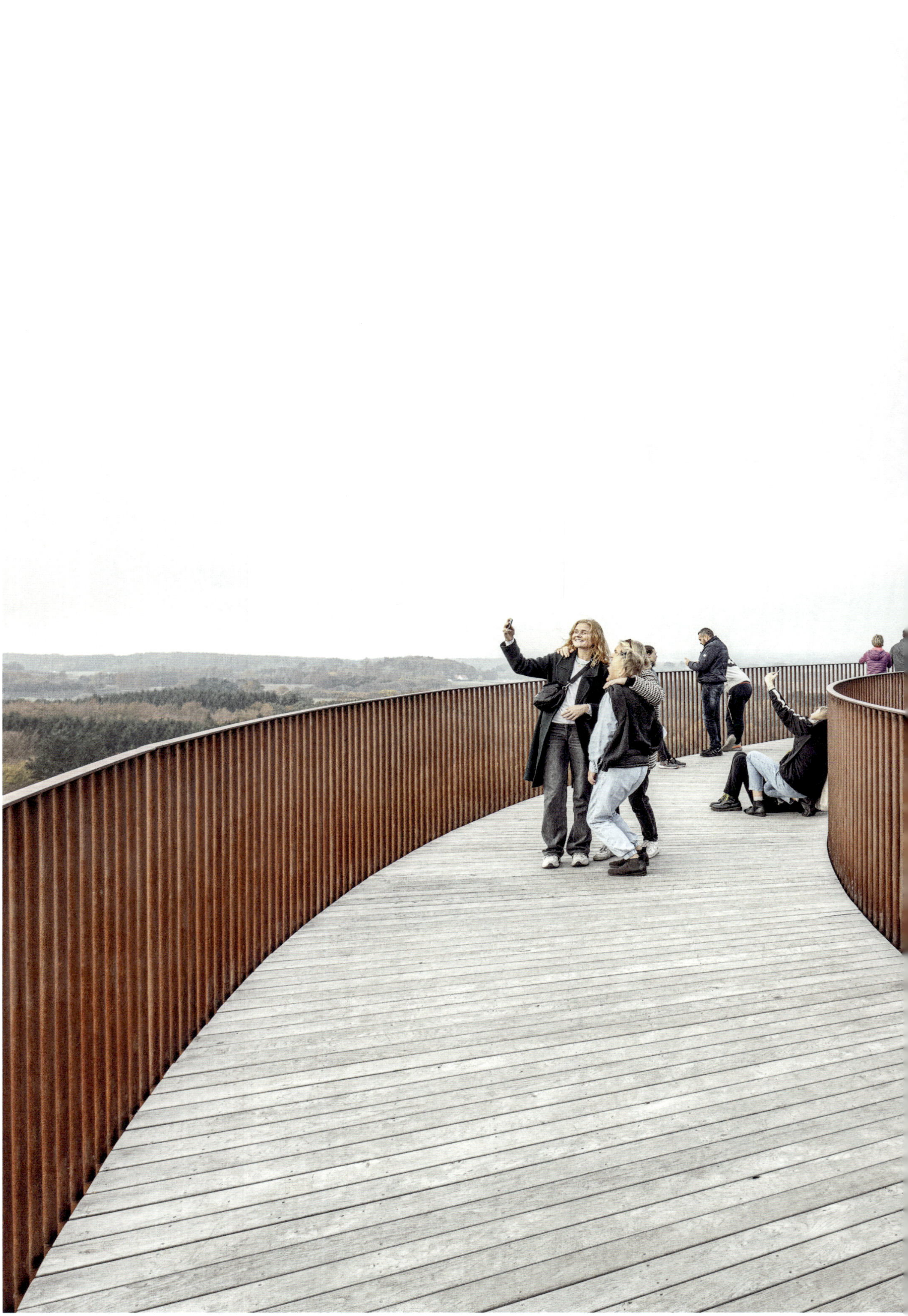

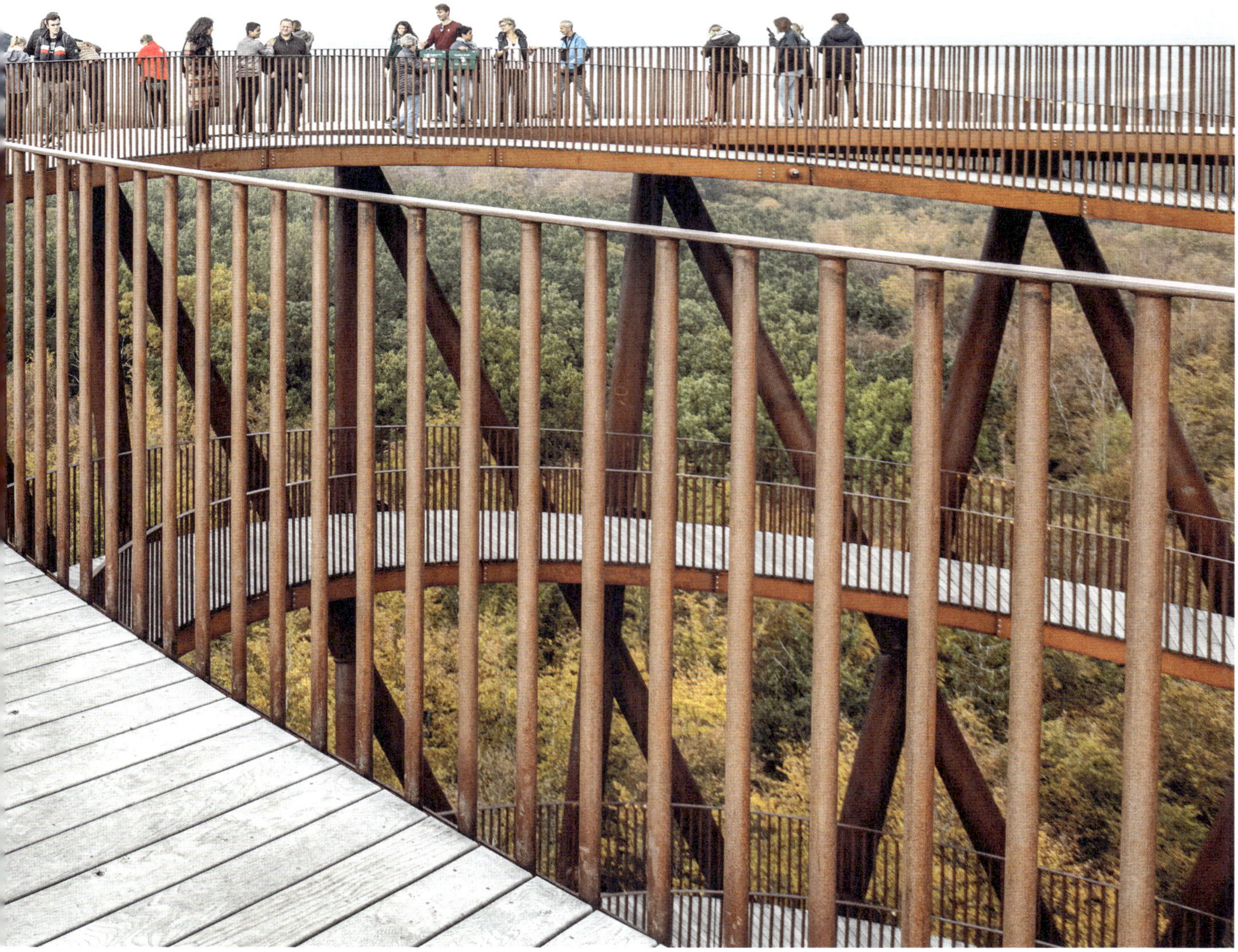

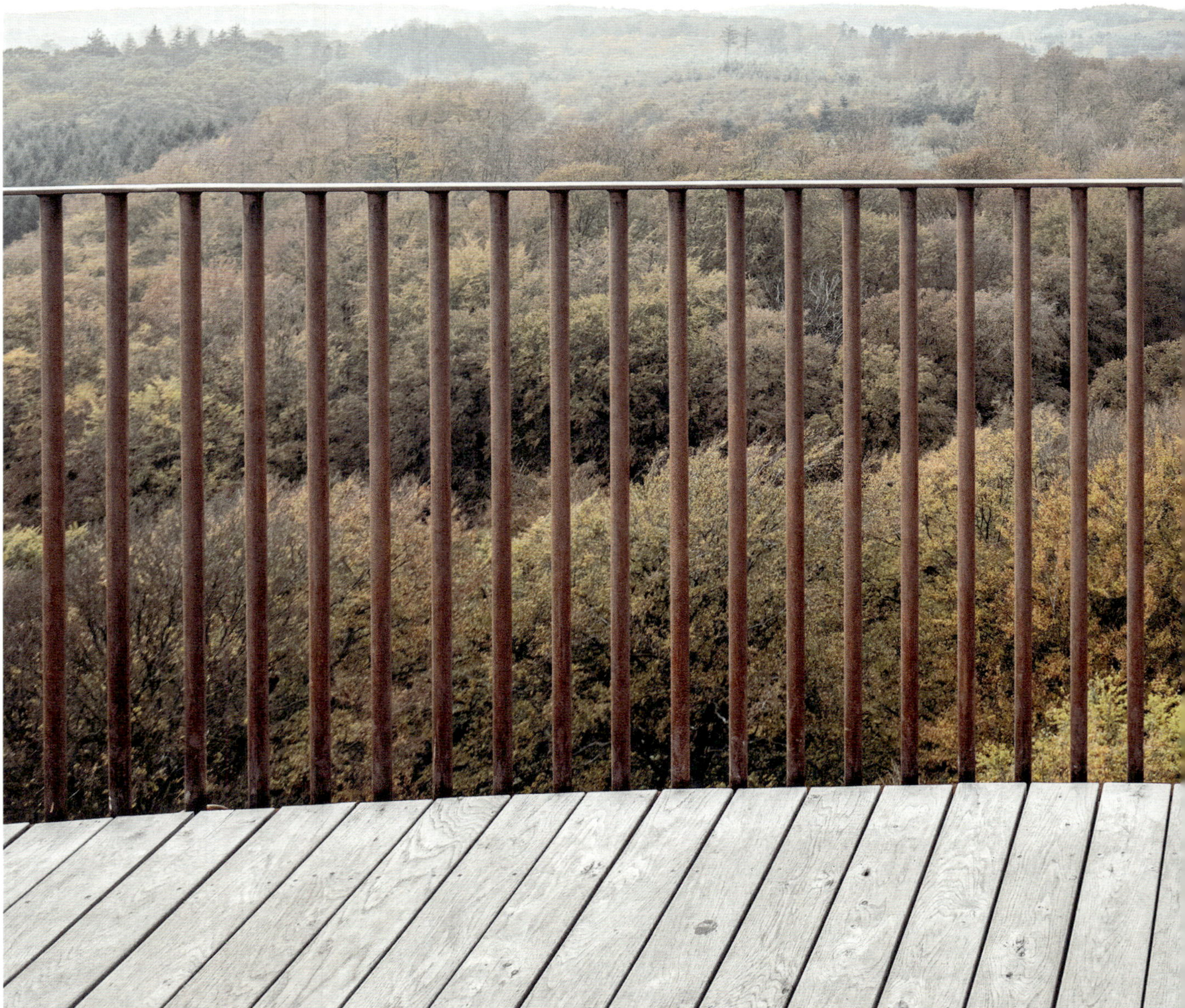

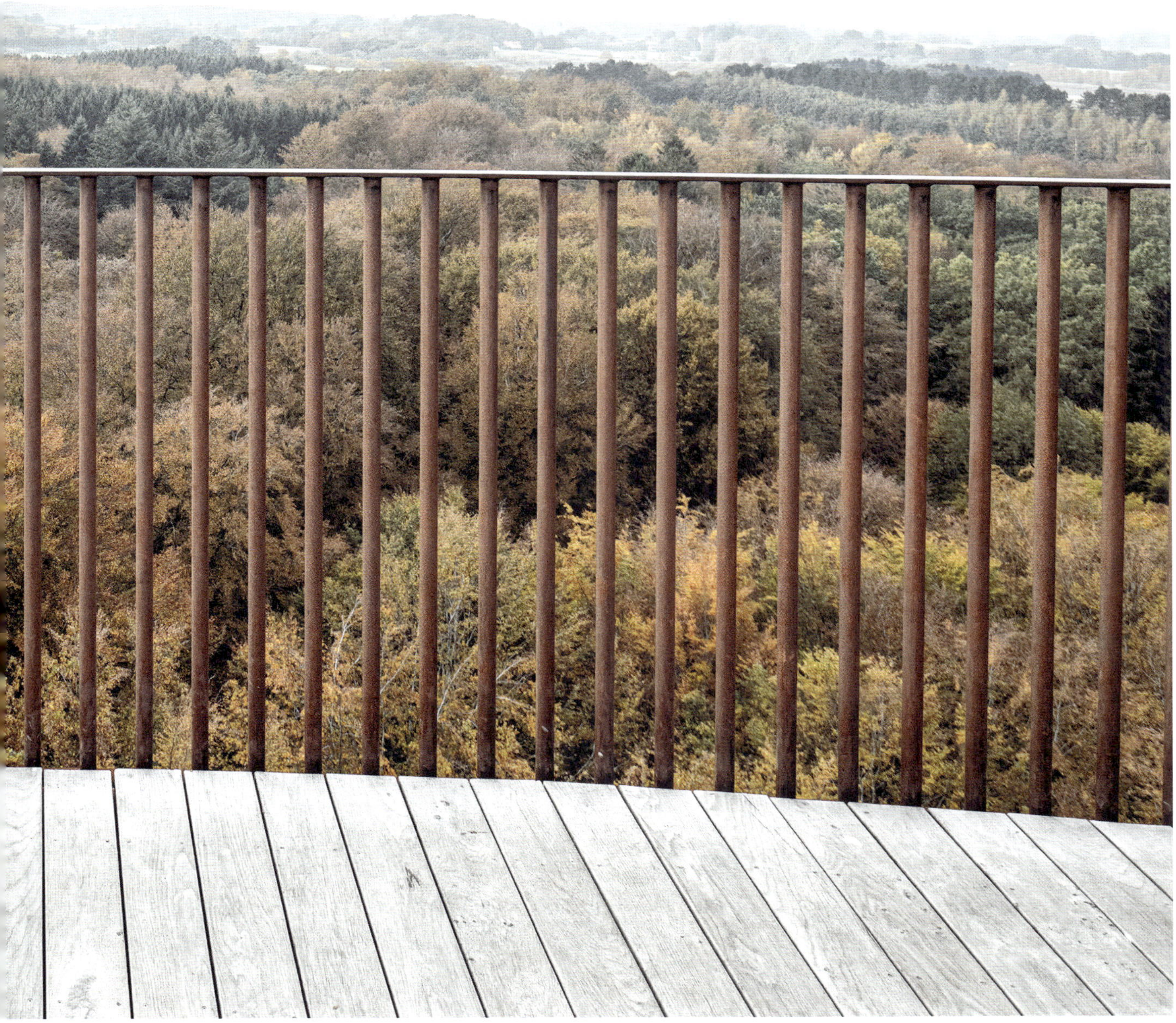

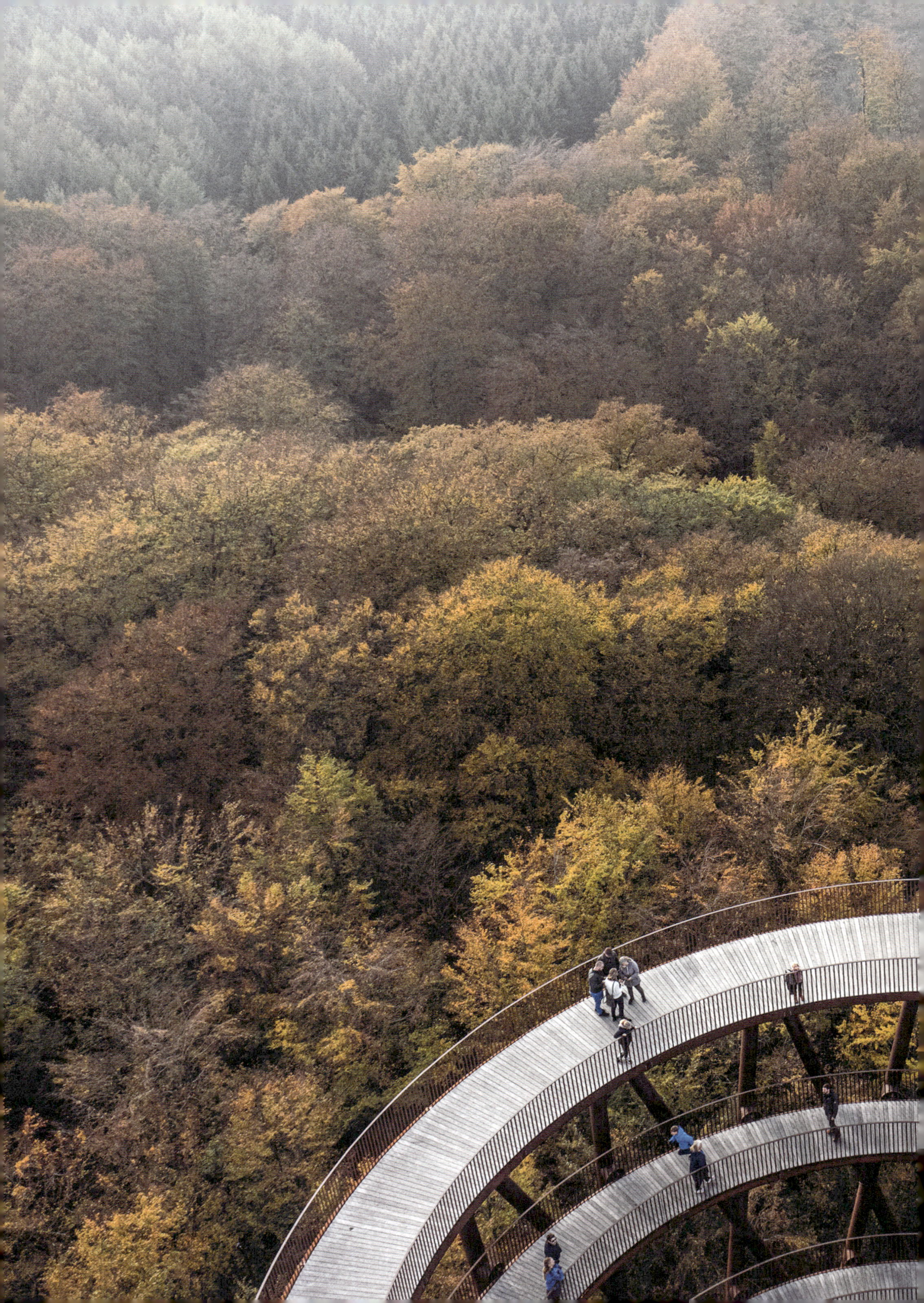

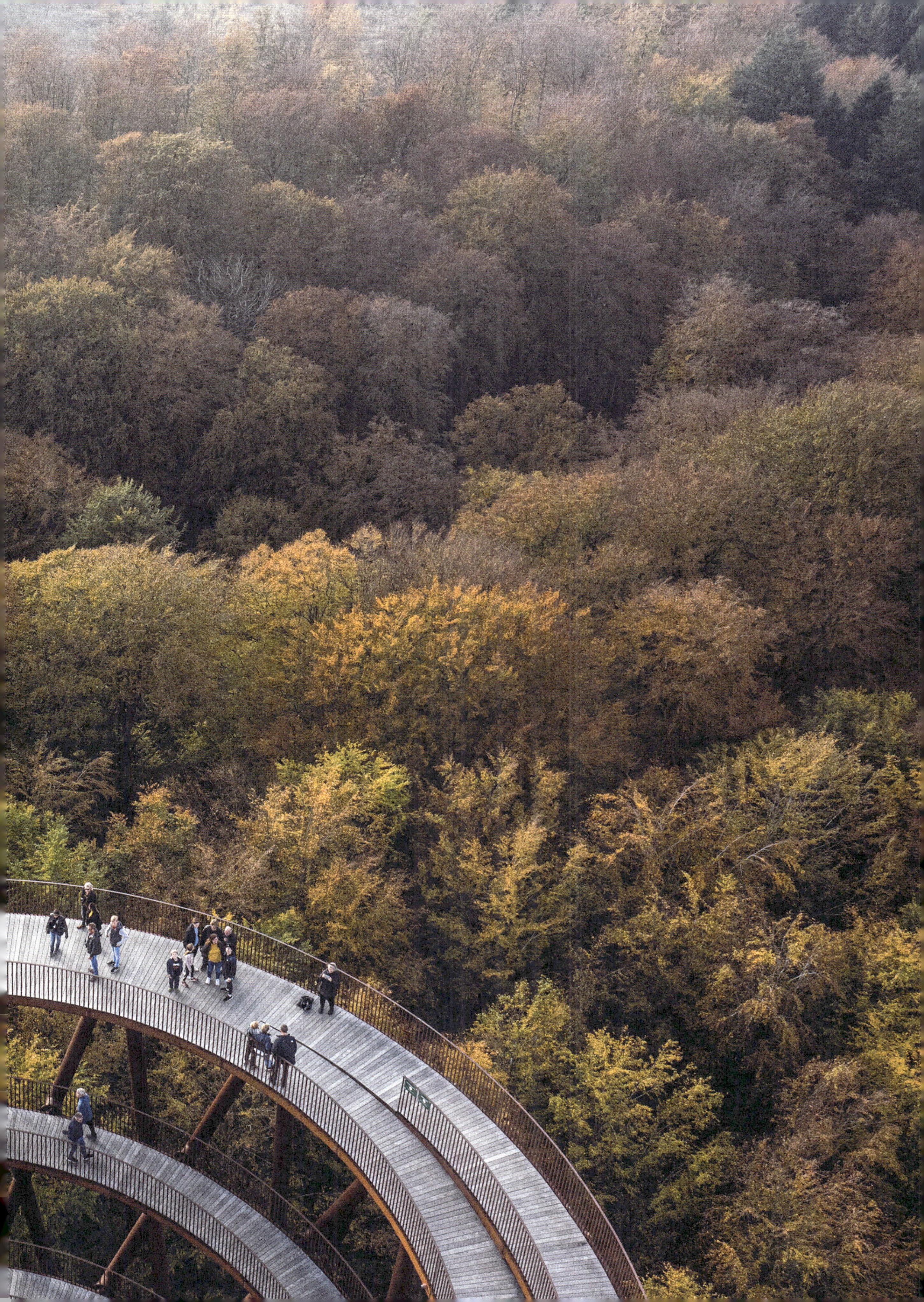

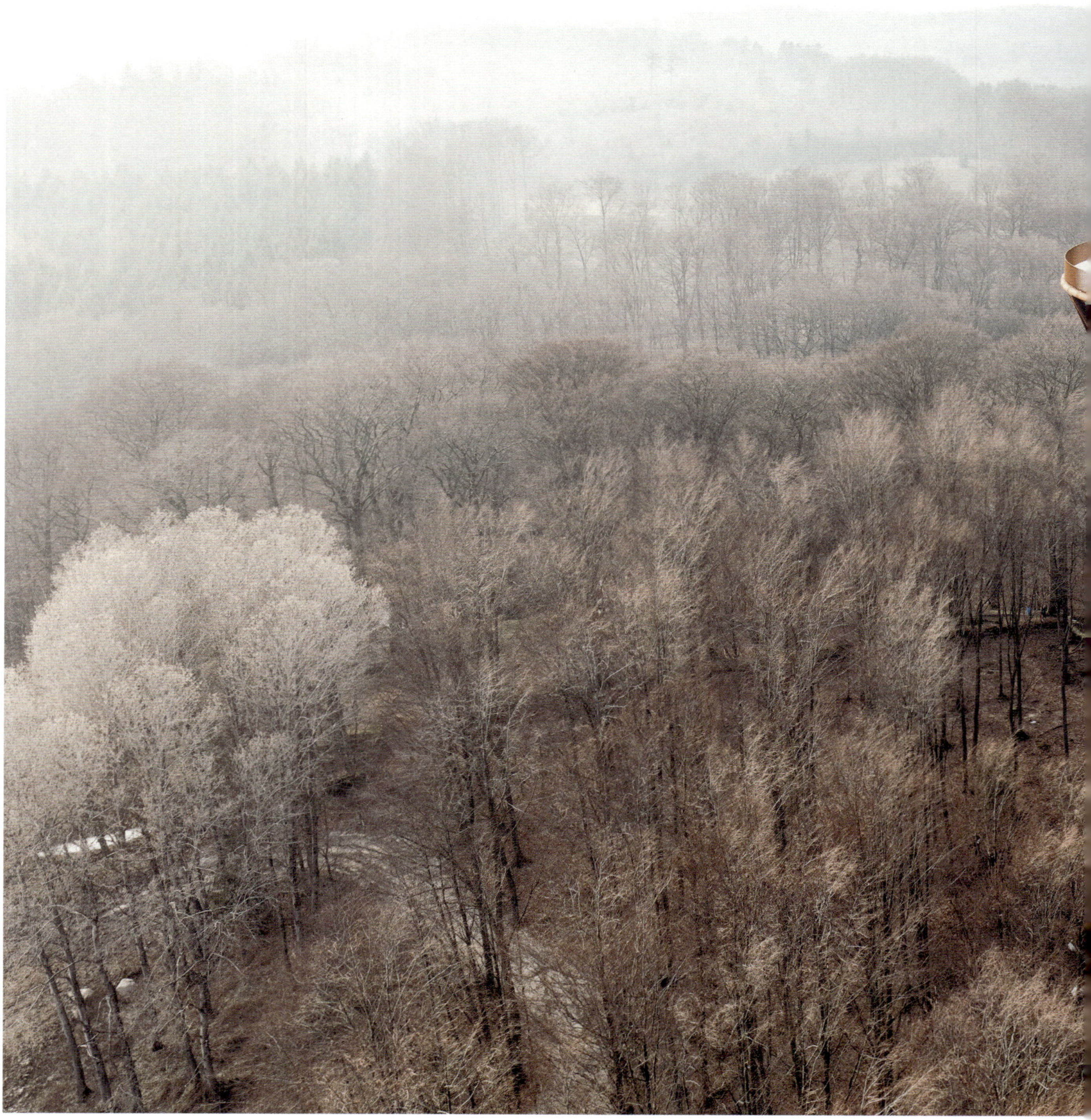

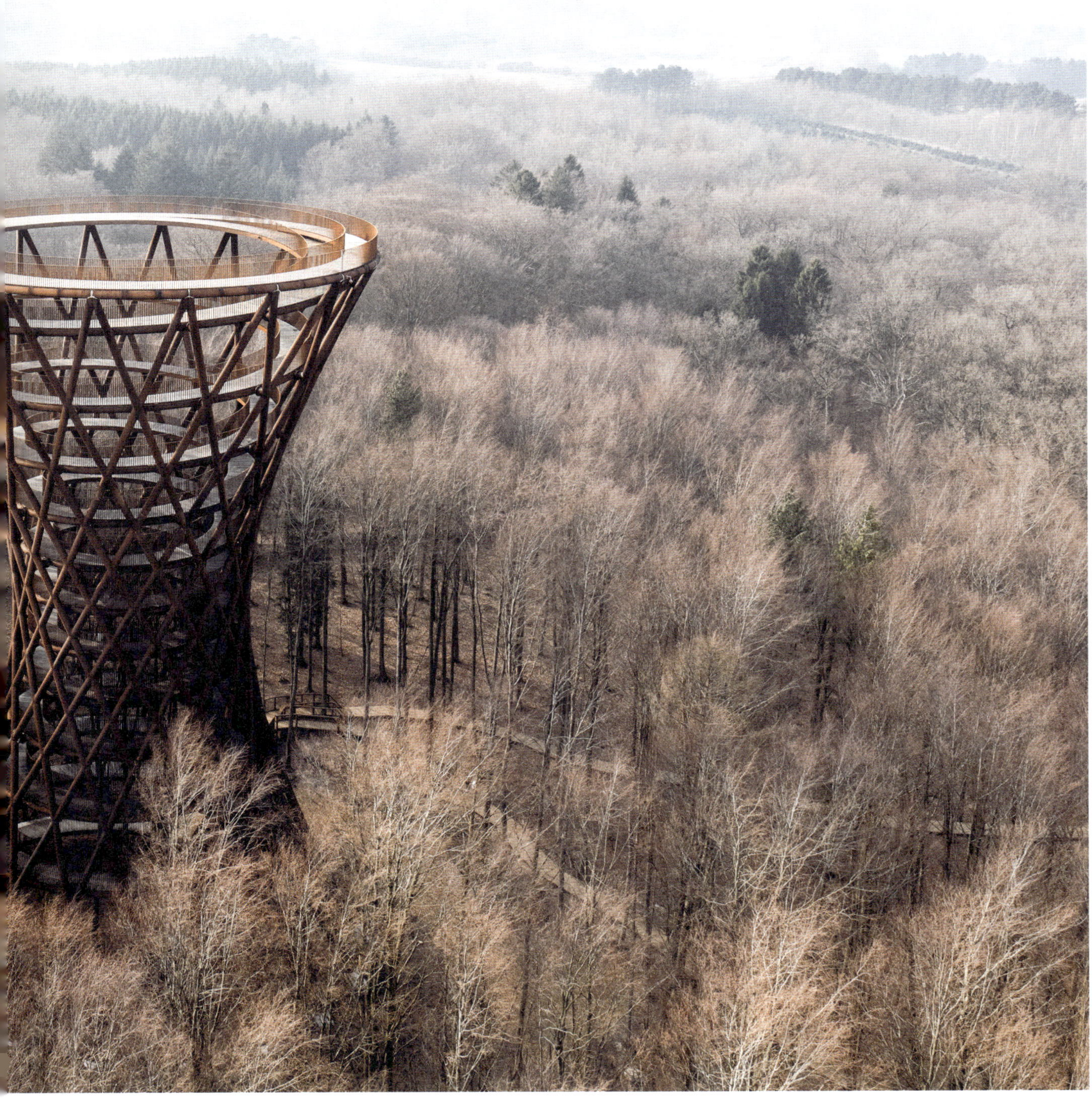

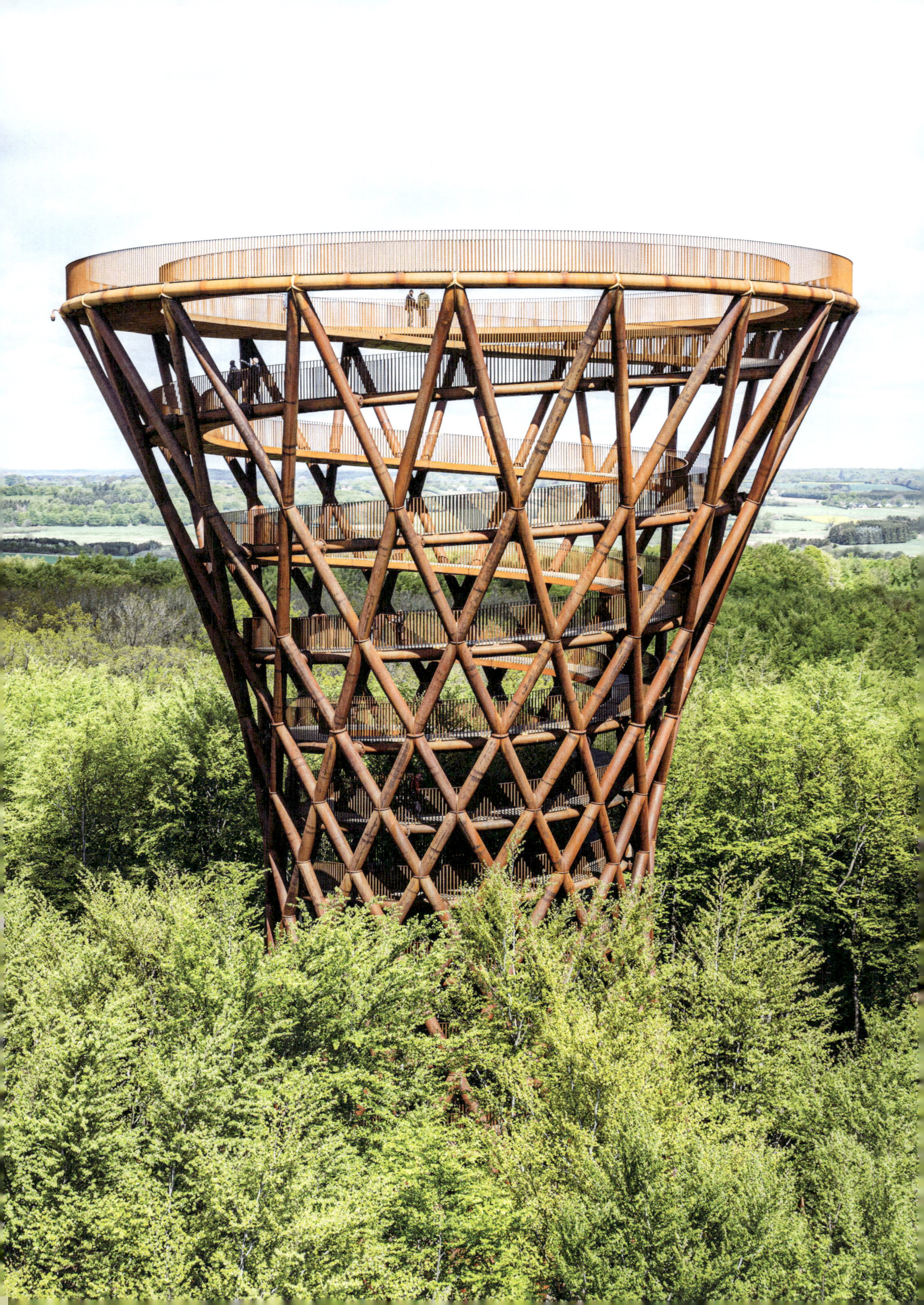

A Tower in the Landscape

By Kristoffer Lindhardt Weiss and Kasper Larsen

In the wood Denderup Vænge on southern Zealand, on the estate of the former monastery Gisselfeld Kloster, the private client Camp Adventure has created an attraction that has transformed the landscape in several ways. Since 2013, Camp Adventure has been turning the area into a destination that attracts visitors from near and far. The latest attraction is the Forest Tower, designed by EFFEKT Architects, and together with the many other activities in the wood, it has put the area on the map and become a beacon of development on southern Zealand. International media outlets, including the American TV network CBS and the German news medium *Der Spiegel*, have visited Gisselfeld to tell the story of the project. This attention is evidence of the Forest Tower's unparalleled contribution to the promotion of what was once a somewhat forgotten spot in the Danish countryside. The Forest Tower challenges our notions of what is possible and reminds us that nature, a scarce resource, is one of our most valuable assets. The success of the project underscores the inherent potential of developing the open land as a real alternative to further expanding the cities. It also speaks to our urge to be in nature and to discover the wide open Danish landscape that offers a contrast to the endless suburban sprawl. The Forest Tower opens our gaze to the qualities contained in the long geological history and the grandeur of the open landscape.

Camp Adventure is situated on one of the main farms at Gisselfeld, the former mill farm Brødebækgaard. In the light, airy beech forests surrounding the farm we find Brødebækken, the stream that waters the lush woods and surrounding lands. The Renaissance castle and park of Gisselfeld Kloster is situated in the middle of the southern Zealand landscape as a striking testimony of the region's century-long historic significance. The name Gisselfeld can be traced all the way back to 1370, but the red building compound found on the site today was constructed from 1547 to 1575 by Peder Oxe, the Steward of the Realm. The castle's landscaped grounds are an integral part of the overall impression the visitor takes away. The castle and the Forest Tower tie history together as two poles of the story about a unique place in Denmark, both highlighting core qualities of the nature and culture they are a part of.

As owner of the forest that forms the setting of the project, Jens Risom, CEO and manager of Gisselfeld Kloster, played a key role in realizing the Forest Tower. Risom explains, 'We regard the forest as a resource with a potential that goes beyond the production of timber and Christmas trees and its role as hunting grounds that most estates rely on. Virtually all Danish woodlands are planted; they are production landscapes that we should not be afraid to modify. We can use nature for a wide range of public activities while also teaching people about nature. This is a way of tapping into a new business potential as part of the expe-

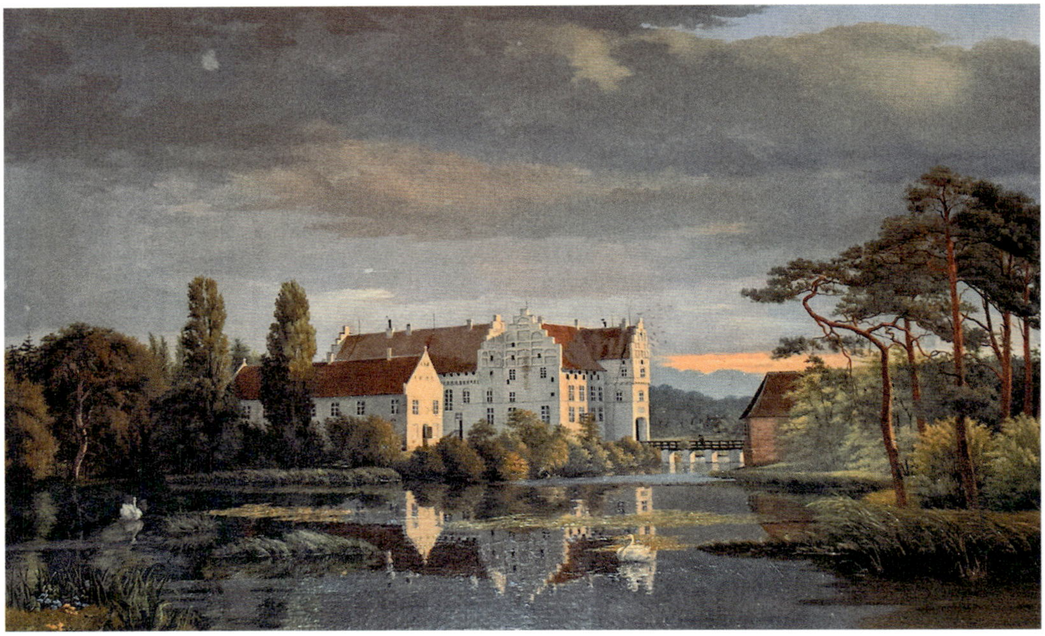

Gisselfeld, C. V. M. Jensen, 1839.

rience economy. Jesper and Camp Adventure were quick to spot this potential, and as early as 2013 they began to create projects that activate the forest. Of course, there is a particular motivation in finding products that have beneficial spinoff effects for the greater local area and make it an even more attractive location for people to move to. I often say that we now have three icons at Gisselfeld Kloster: the 16th-century castle itself, the conservatory and the Forest Tower. The tower has become part of our brand. In the past, the manor was said to be the main engine of the local community, and today, we are seeing the same dynamic in play. We are helping to bring more activity, awareness and jobs to our local area.' The local moorings of the project are a reminder of the importance of the commitment passionate local players can bring to the otherwise technical and heavily bureaucratic decision-making processes that often characterize ambitious construction projects. 'This type of project is only possible with the engagement of people and authorities that see the possibilities before the limitations. The local department of the Danish Nature Agency, Storstrøm, was a very constructive interlocutor with a keen understanding that trust and entrepreneurship must go hand in hand. The then Mayor, Knud Erik Hansen, and Thomas Eriksen, then Chief Executive of Faxe Municipality, were important cooperation partners who shared our commitment to promoting the area and the larger region as a tourist destination. At the Danish Nature Agency, we had the pleasure of working with Forest Supervisor Claus Jespersen. Claus has an agile and innovative mind; he sees the value of projects that offer physical experiences and is able to embrace different perspectives on forests. The forest is protected against changes in land use, which means building permits are rarely granted. It

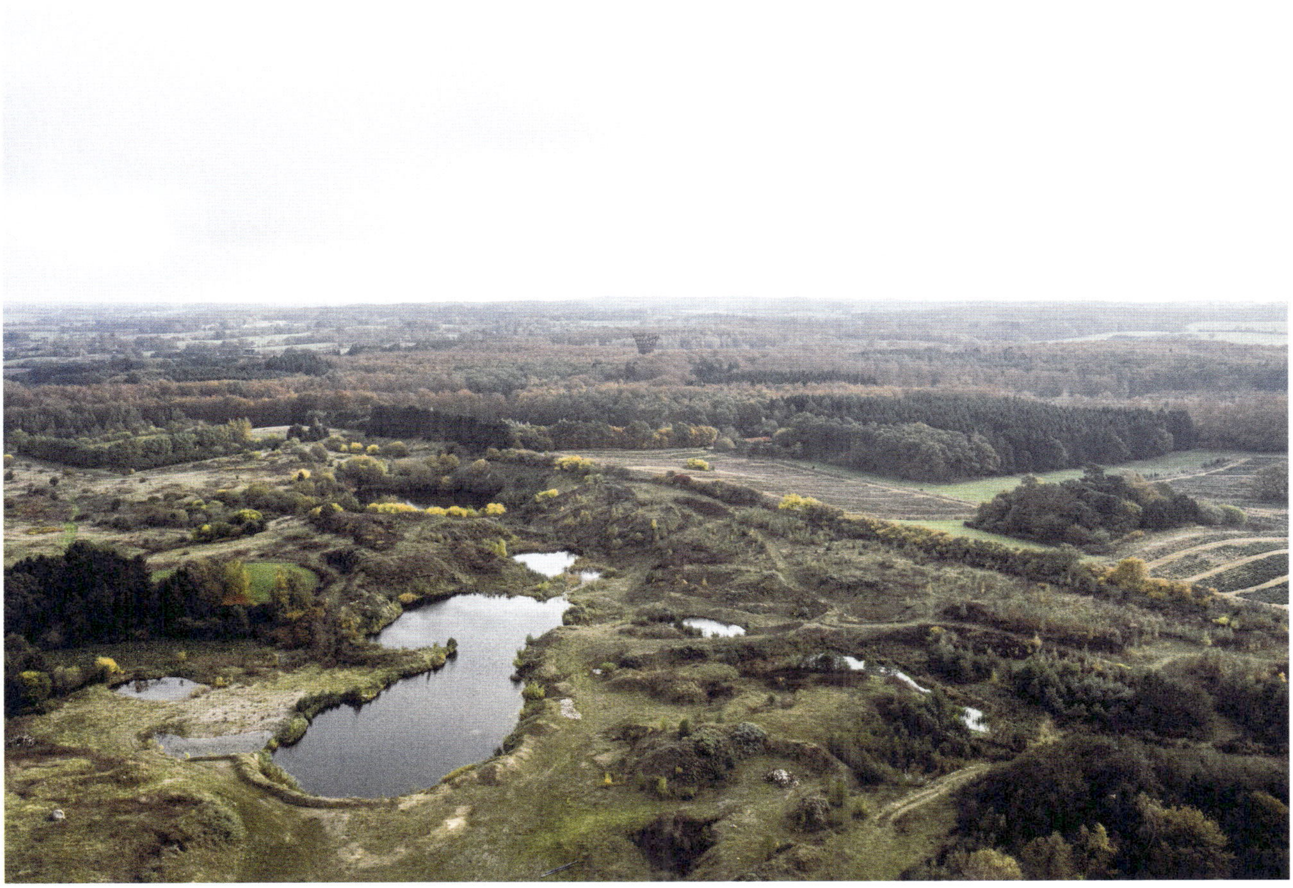

The Forest Tower is located in a landscape shaped by the Ice Age.

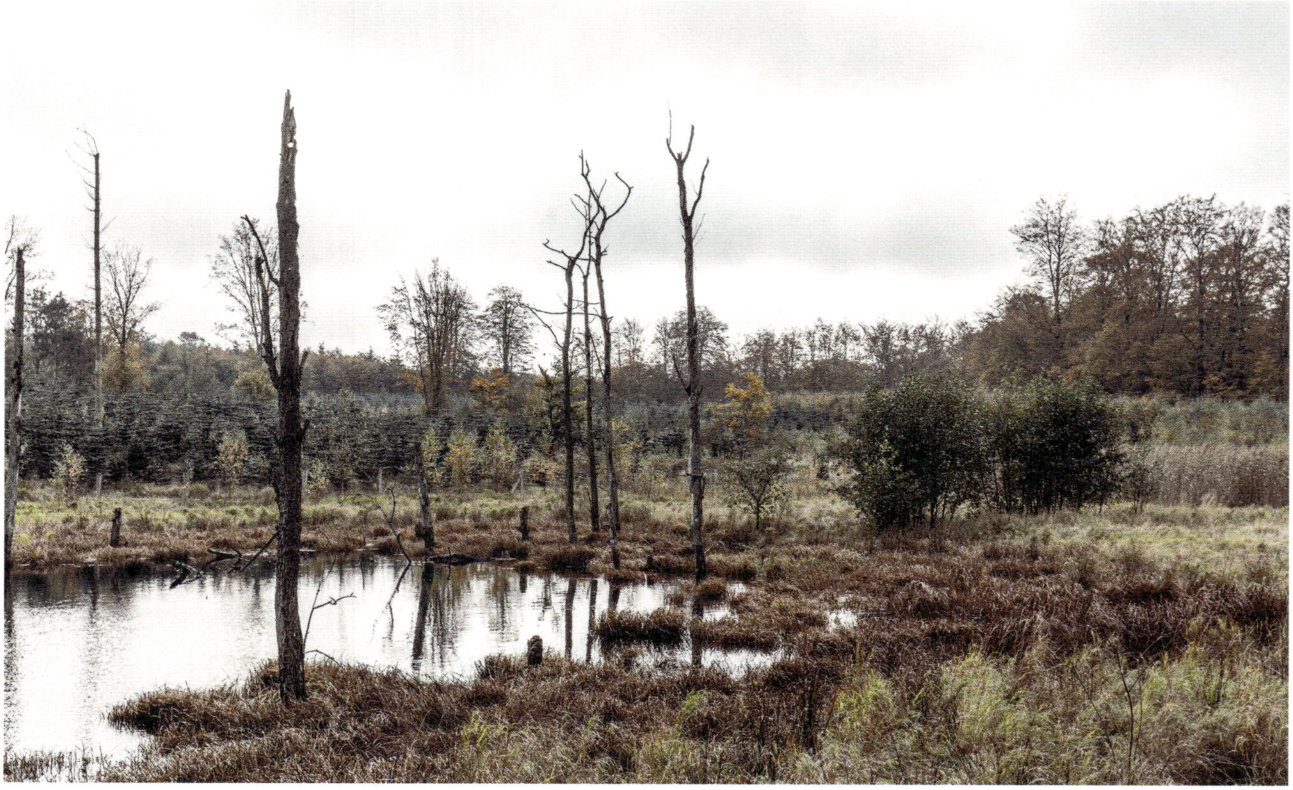

The natural scenery surrounding the tower consists of varied landscape types.

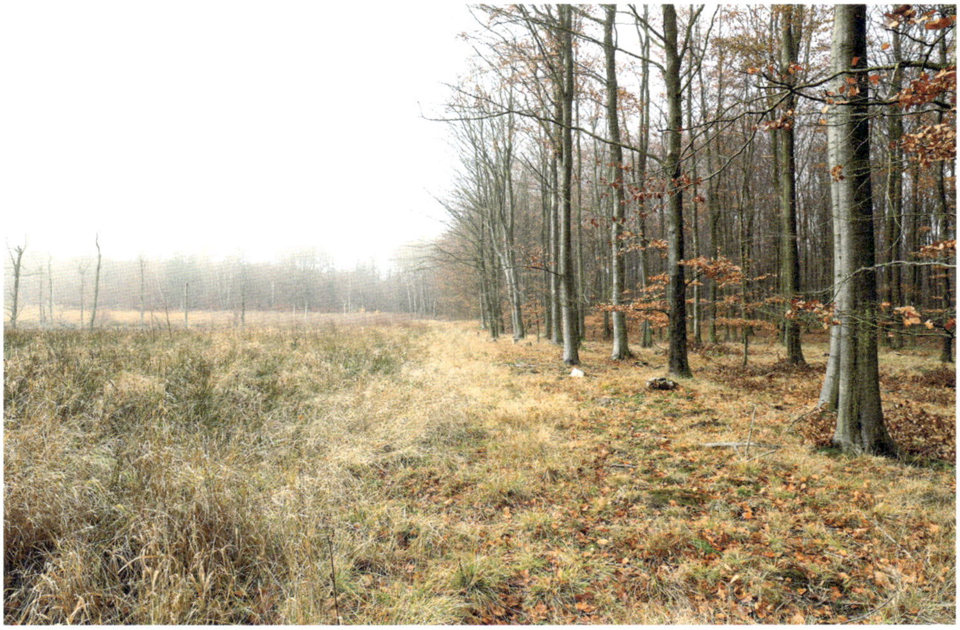

Deciduous forest and open fields.

is not a reserve, as many people think, but in early 1805, when only about 2% of Denmark was forested, a law was passed that protected the Danish forests. The restrictions that were introduced still apply to this day, and thus, normally, the only buildings that are allowed are ones that have an operational purpose. There was an alternative project proposal that would have placed the tower outside the forest itself, but the project only has value to the visitors if it is situated inside the forest. Ultimately, we got permission to build a 60-metre-tall tower, and the resulting impact of tourism-related activities has highlighted the fact that development in rural districts is often cumbersome and slow due to different types of legislation that block the realization of good projects. Once the tower was completed, the Environmental Protection Agency and the Danish Nature Agency came here on their annual summer excursion for the staff in order to learn more about how to introduce commercial tourism activities inside a forest. They spend large sums of money in the forest districts they oversee, but they are short on funds. The Forest Tower demonstrates the feasibility of creating a new source of revenue that does not destroy the forest. The two agencies saw this as an interesting project and a driver of development that might be used as an example in other locations.'

That is the key lesson from the Forest Tower project. The tower demonstrates a sensitive adaptation to the landscape and the long, rich history of nature and culture that shaped it. In doing so, it revitalizes these qualities to promote Danish tourism. The means of this revitalization is a world-class architectural solution that received awards for its spectacular design even before the project was completed. The combination of the unique landscape and a signature design that both highlights and contributes to its setting has made the Forest Tower an international success story that far exceeds initial expectations.

Together with other destinations, the Forest Tower has already led to an increase in the number of tourists visiting the region. The project has brought cultural and natural history into the modern experience economy and reshaped our mental landscape. During the first year, Camp Adventure has had a little over 350,000 visitors, and many people's perception of southern Zealand has changed for good. The inspiration for a viewing tower comes from Germany, where Camp Adventure's founder and director, Jesper Mathiesen, and the business developer Kasper Larsen studied a similar project on the island of Rügen in northern Germany, Naturerbe Zentrum Rügen (Natural Heritage Centre Rügen). The Danish project reflects the fact that although Denmark has thousands of kilometres of coastline, the forests, with their rich wildlife, are the top recreational destination for Danes. By facilitating access to a type of area that, sadly, is rare in Denmark, the project serves a dual purpose: in addition to offering positive experiences, it strengthens our connection to the nature of southern Zealand and promotes a deeper understanding of our cultural history.

The undulating Ice Age landscape

Over a brief period, the Forest Tower has welcomed a large number of visitors who have taken in the view of the old forest itself and a vast swathe of the landscape of southern Zealand from the top of the 45-metre-tall tower. The characteristic undulating Ice Age landscape has few parallels anywhere in the world. Expansive outwash plains, deep gullies, the impressive glacial ridge with river valleys slowly winding their way towards the sea, gentle rolling hills and the farmland of historical estates lie spread out like a canvas showing the impact of time. All part of the magnificent moraine landscape that forms the setting for the Forest Tower and which has been cultivated and occupied since early settlers began to clear woodlands more than 6,000 years ago. The landscape's current form was moulded by the most recent ice age some 15,000 years ago. The powerful forces of the ice pushed and carved out hills and valleys to form a so-called dead-ice landscape, as exemplified by the lands west of the nearby village of Rønnede. Here springs the source of Susåen, the largest river in southern Zealand. The Ice Age glaciers gradually covered and then retreated from southern Zealand over a period from about 18,000 BCE to about 10,000 BCE. This process created the varied landscape that can only fully be appreciated from the viewing platform at the top of the spiral-shaped tower. At 140 metres above sea level, the viewing platform is the highest accessible point on Zealand. On a clear day, the view extends for 25 km in all directions. All the way to the Øresund bridge, southern Sweden, the Turning Torso building in Malmö and parts of the Copenhagen skyline towards the north-east. Thus, the Forest Tower not only offers a closer look at the local area but also a panoramic view of large swaths of Zealand.

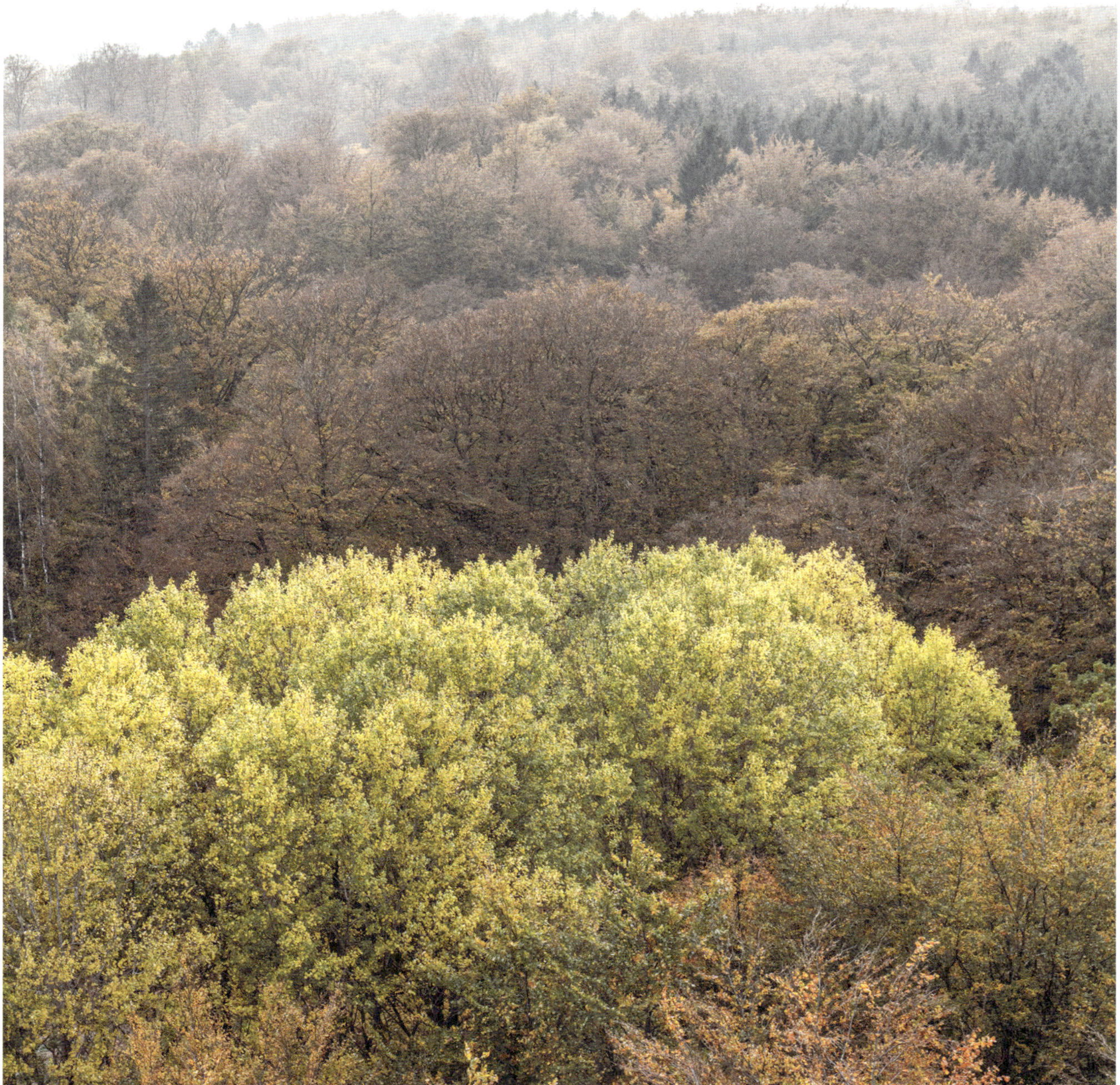

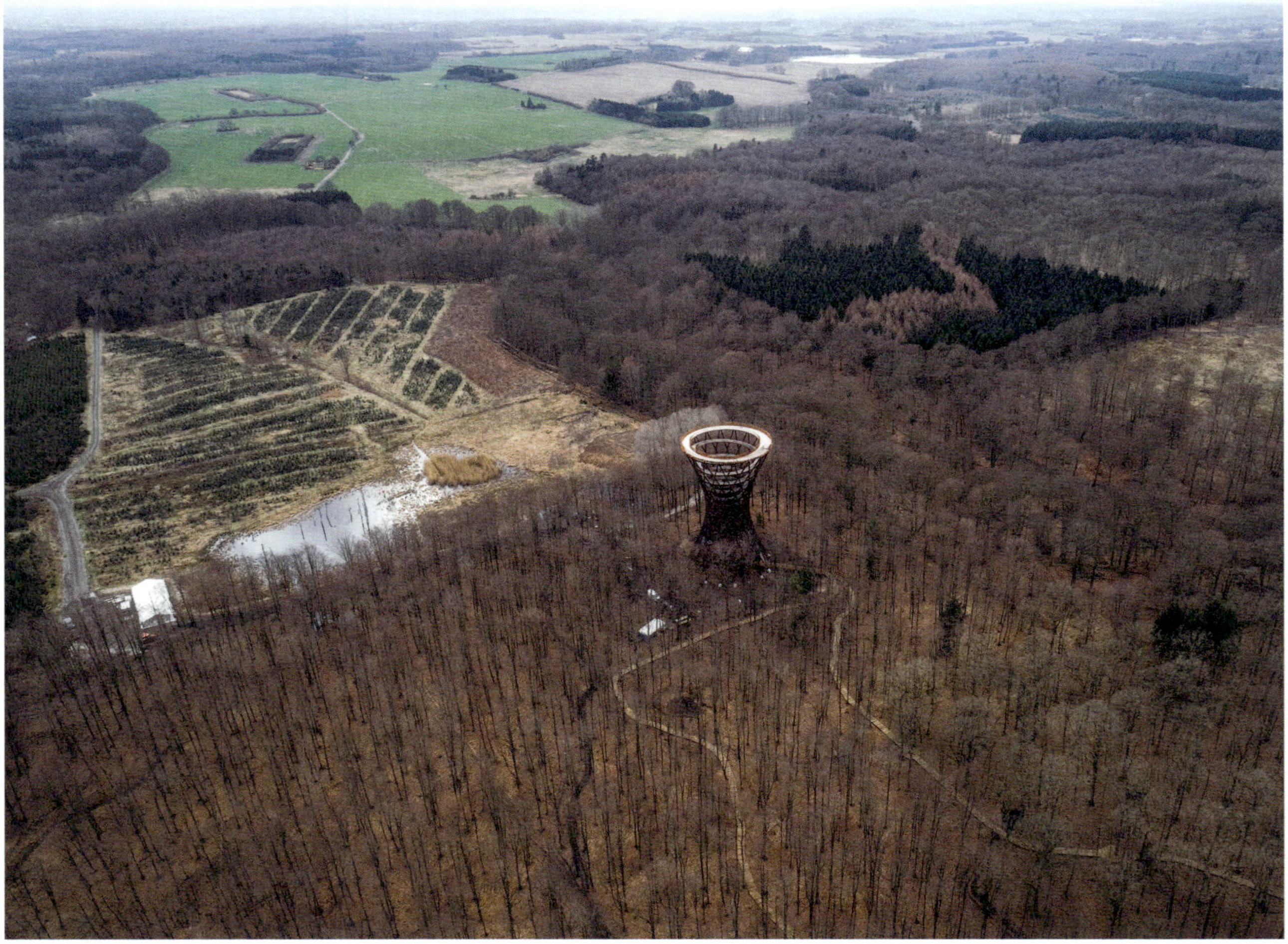

The monumental Forest Tower is a distinctive landmark in the landscape of southern Zealand.

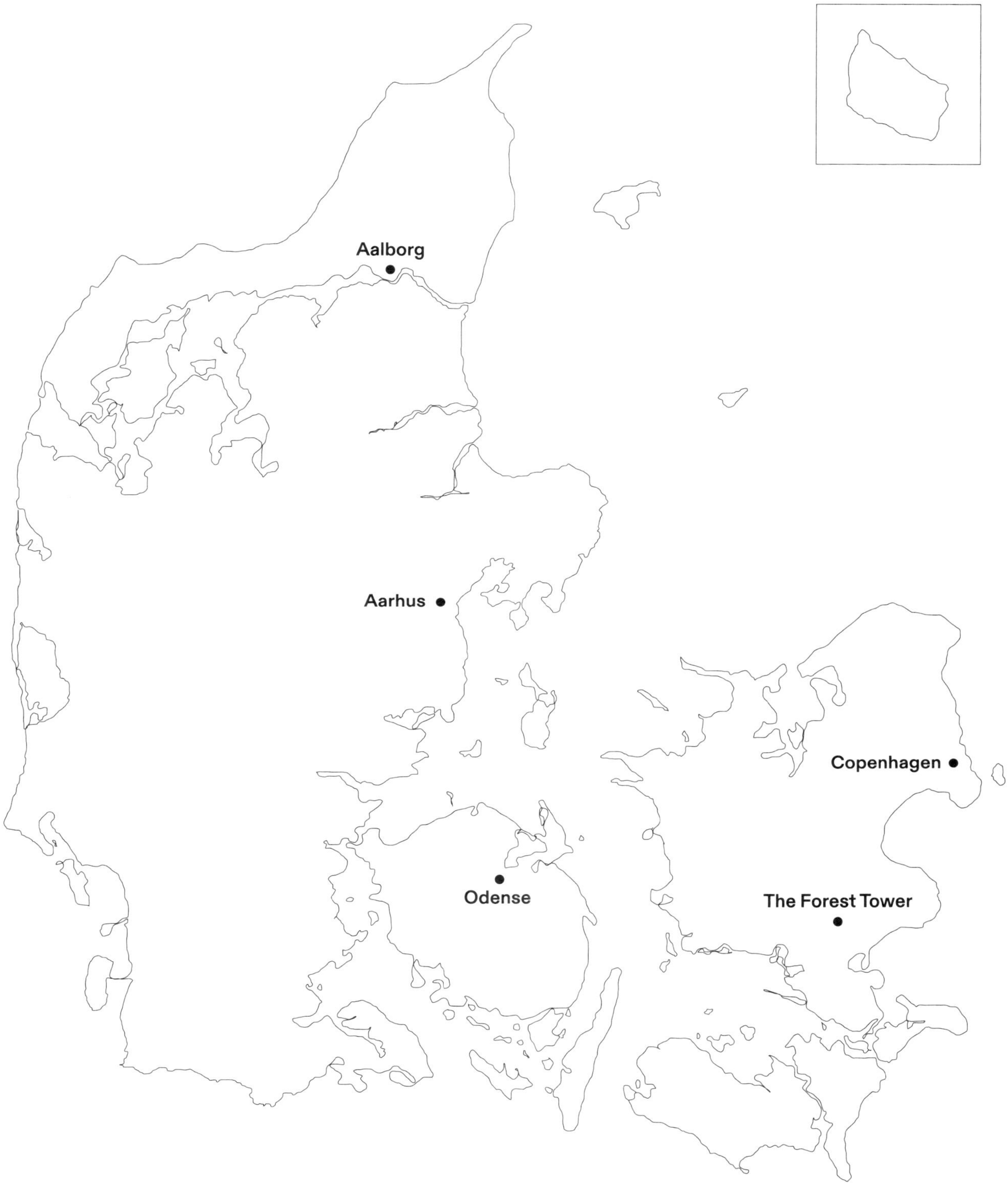

The Forest Tower is situated in southern Zealand.

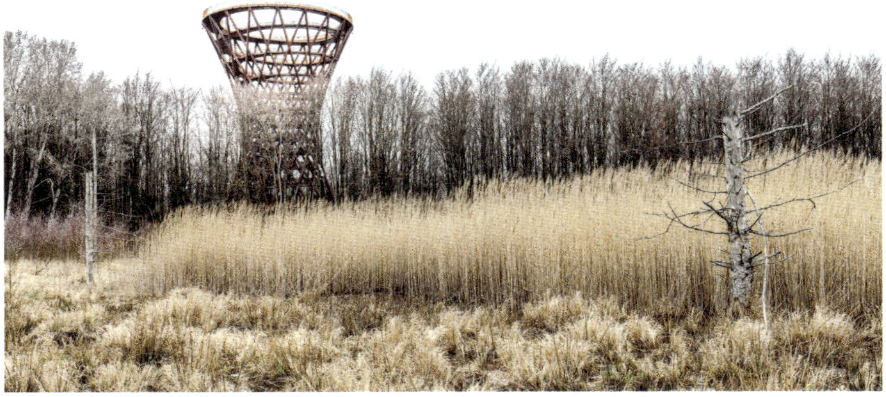

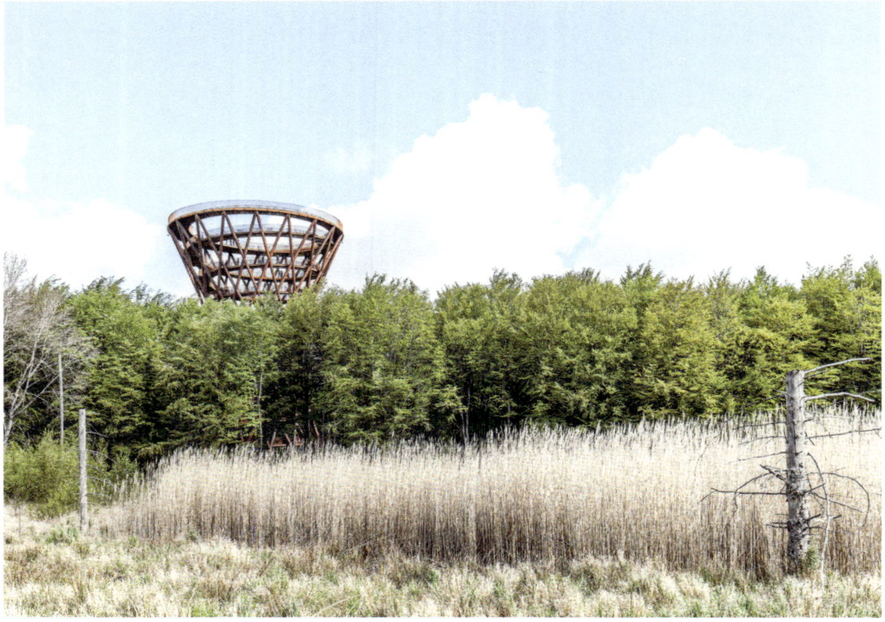

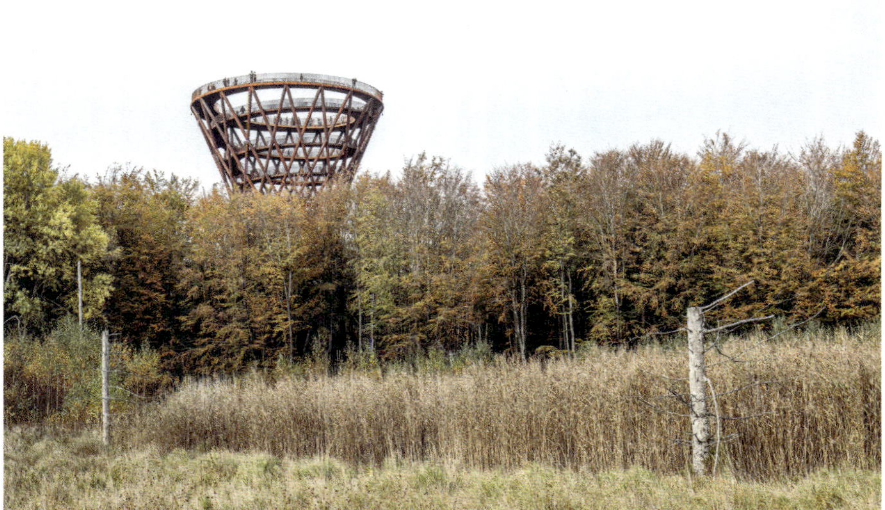

About the Forest Tower

The tower itself has a minimal footprint on the site. The construction respects the character of the place and the nature it has become an integrated part of. From their arrival at Brødebækgaard, visitors follow a 900-metre-long, elevated footpath winding its way among the trees of the forest to the tower. The path is deliberately designed to move around and respect the trees with minimal interference. After guiding visitors past a forest stream, a climbing park and the old trees that define the scene of the spectacular experience, the path continues as a spiral-shaped ramp inside the Forest Tower that invites visitors to climb to the top. All the way up the spiral pathway, visitors are close to the majestic trees gradually ascending to see the tree crowns at eye level and finally arriving to the overwhelming view at the top. The movement inside the tower construction offers a simultaneous sense of gravity and openness. The dimensions of the construction juxtaposed with the tree trunks create a compelling effect that beckons the visitor up towards the top. From the horizontal plane of the forest floor to a view in among the vertical tree trunks to the slow waving movement and rushing sound of the tree crowns and then further up, above the tree crowns, where the wind has free reins, and then, finally, the viewing platform itself.

The design of the Forest Tower is based on a so-called hyperboloid form constructed of long vertical steel pipes that are not bent but instead rotated 120° to produce the curvy hourglass form. The result is a geometric signature shape that appears light and elegant with a unique expression and a transparent character that blends naturally into the dimensions of the forest. The accomplishment of the project stems from the precision of the concept. Camp Adventure chose to partner up with EFFEKT Architects, and in a successful collaboration they developed a conceptual solution with an iconic clarity that has become a regional landmark. A pared-down, easily decoded form, exemplifying that a simple idea married with a clear architectural expression can create a striking result that attracts widespread attention.

A restricted material palette with an unpretentious and technical character creates a clear-cut figure that highlights its surroundings as much as itself. Due to its colour, transparency and structure, the Forest Tower seems to blend in as one approaches it, and then appears. The load-bearing columns of the construction are similar in thickness to the tree trunks. Despite a subtle, toned-down design that does not disturb the peaceful forest setting, the architecture has a succinctly striking signature with a clear and precise expression. Despite the visible and striking character of the constructive elements, including the large bolts that hold the structure together, visitors are able to experience the forest without distraction. That is, in essence, the source of its success – the honest and straightforward architectural treatment that frames and enhances the forest experience. Of course, there is nothing new about the idea of walking or climbing to a high point to overlook a forest or a landscape; what makes the experience so unique is the totality of impressions from arrival to departure. Although the Forest Tower is not a noisy addition to the forest, it also is not meek or aspiring to be invisible. That makes it an interesting architectural project and a fascinating example of how we can build in the forest without destroying its unique qualities and beauty.

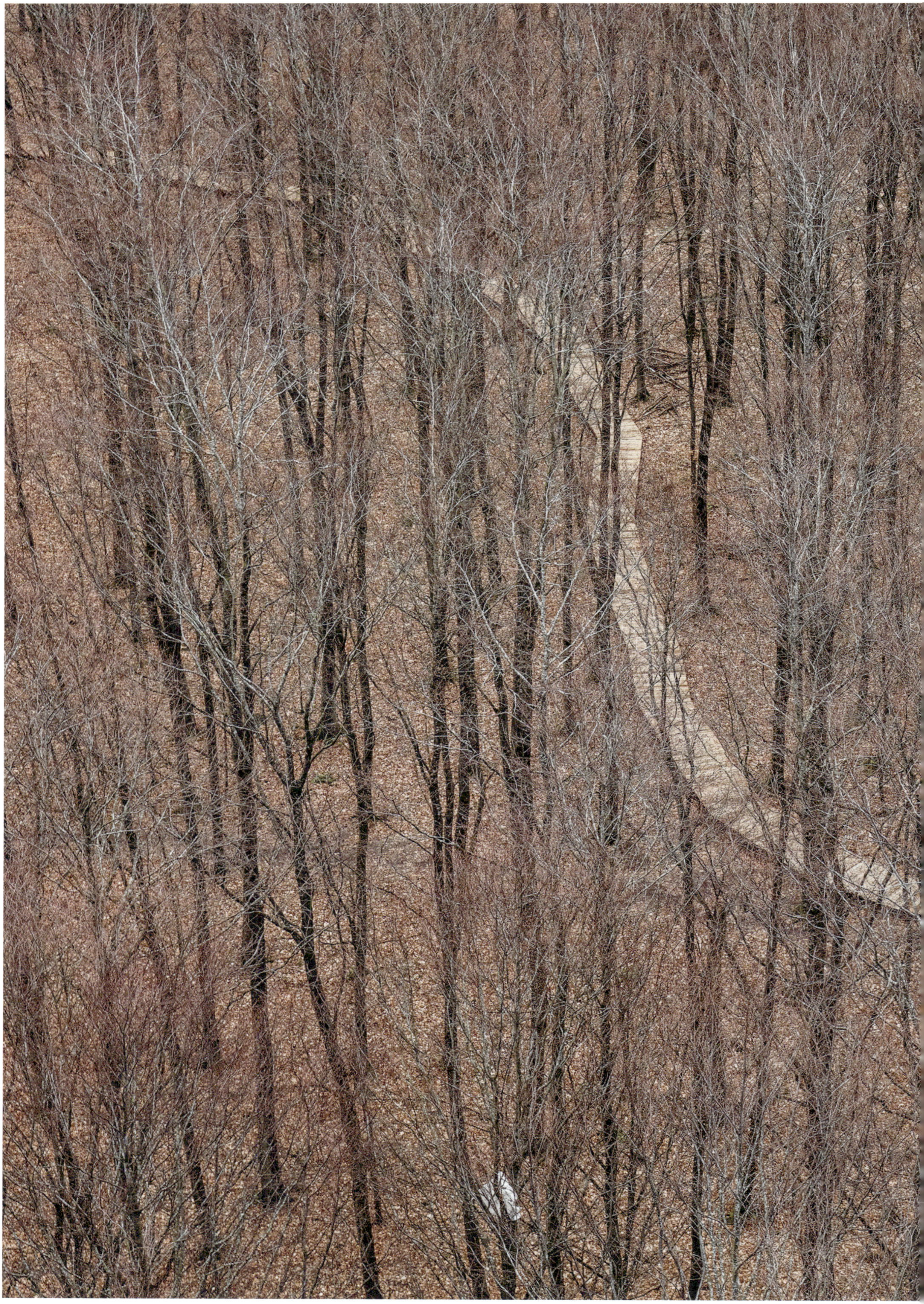

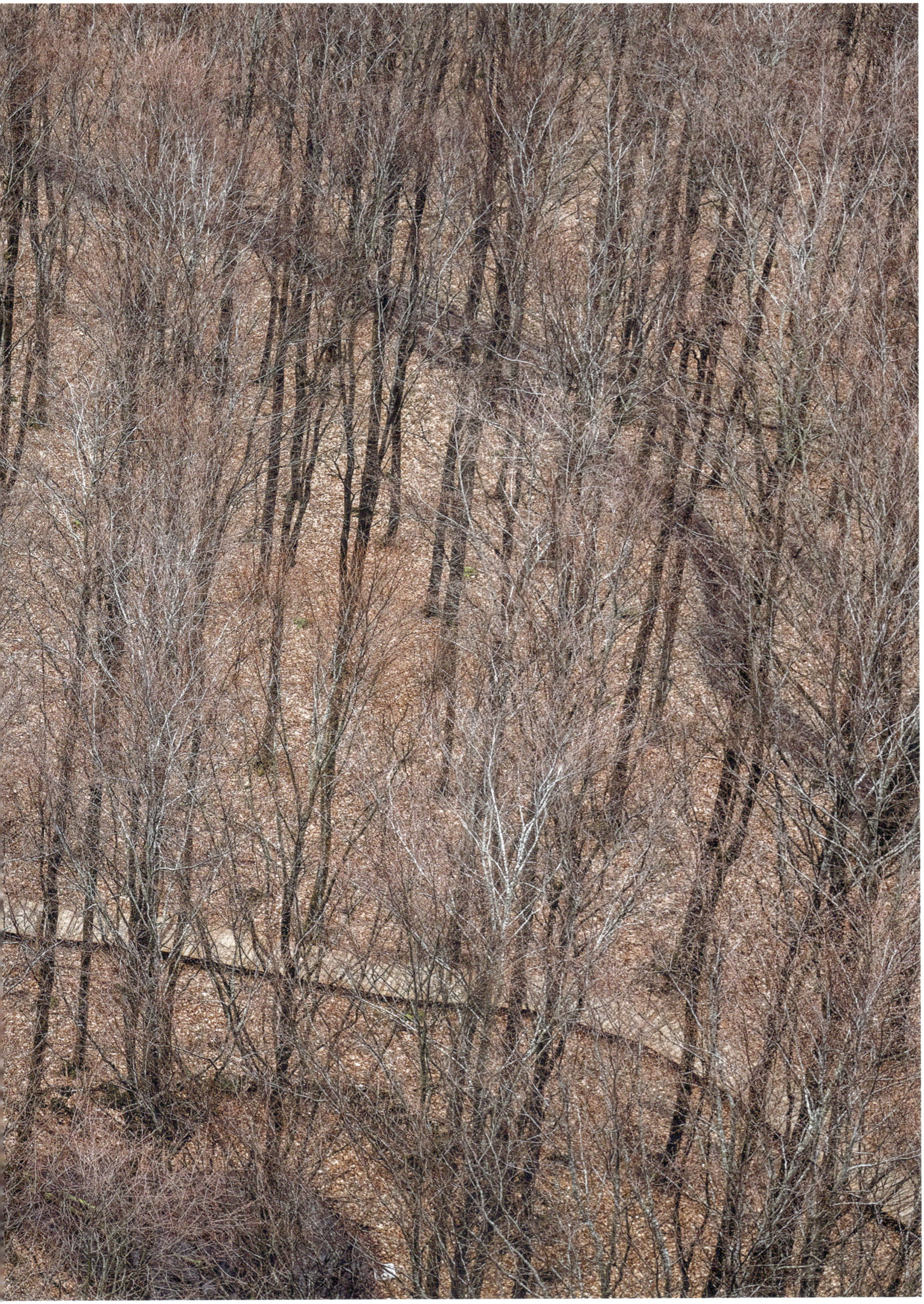

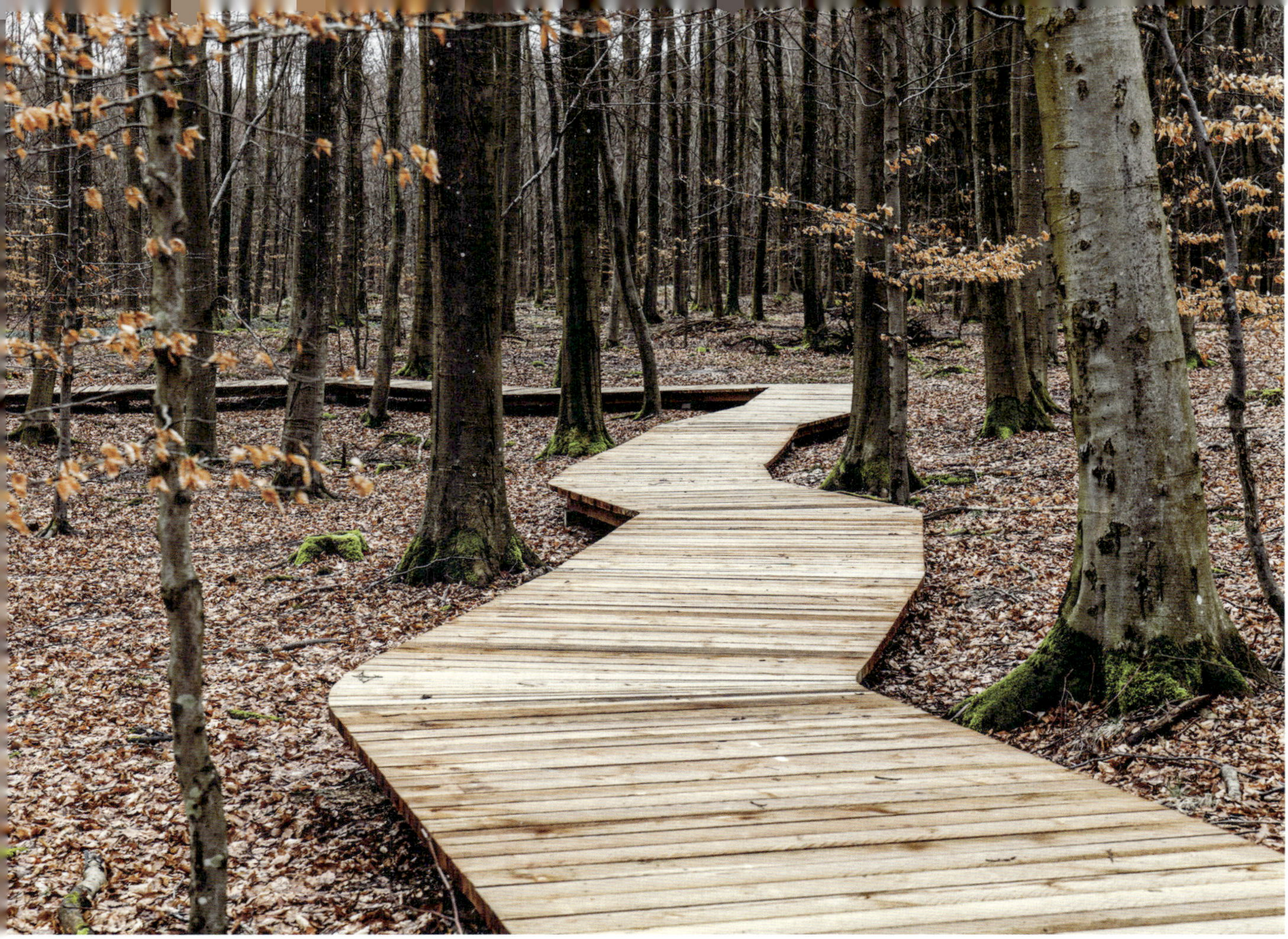

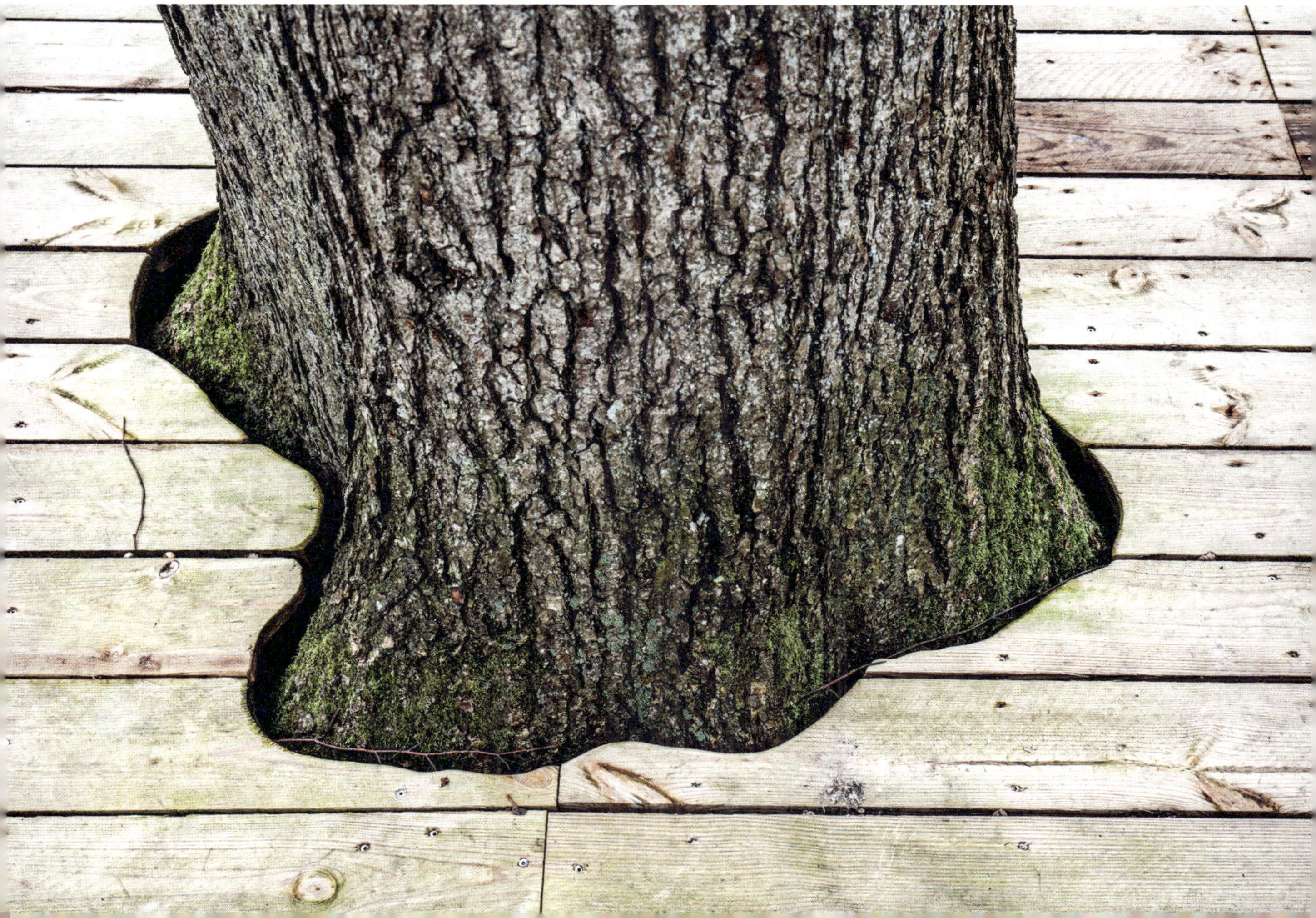

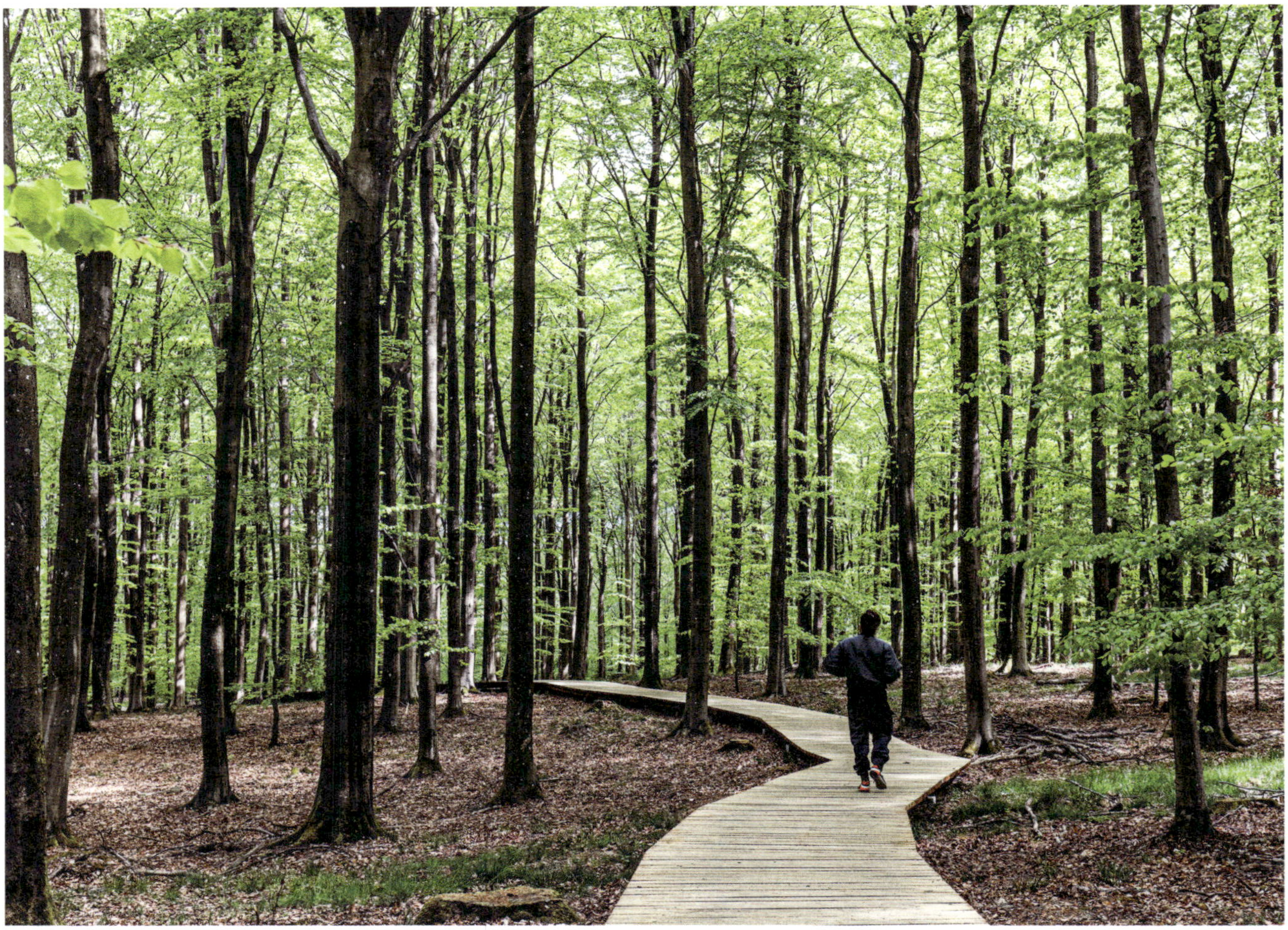

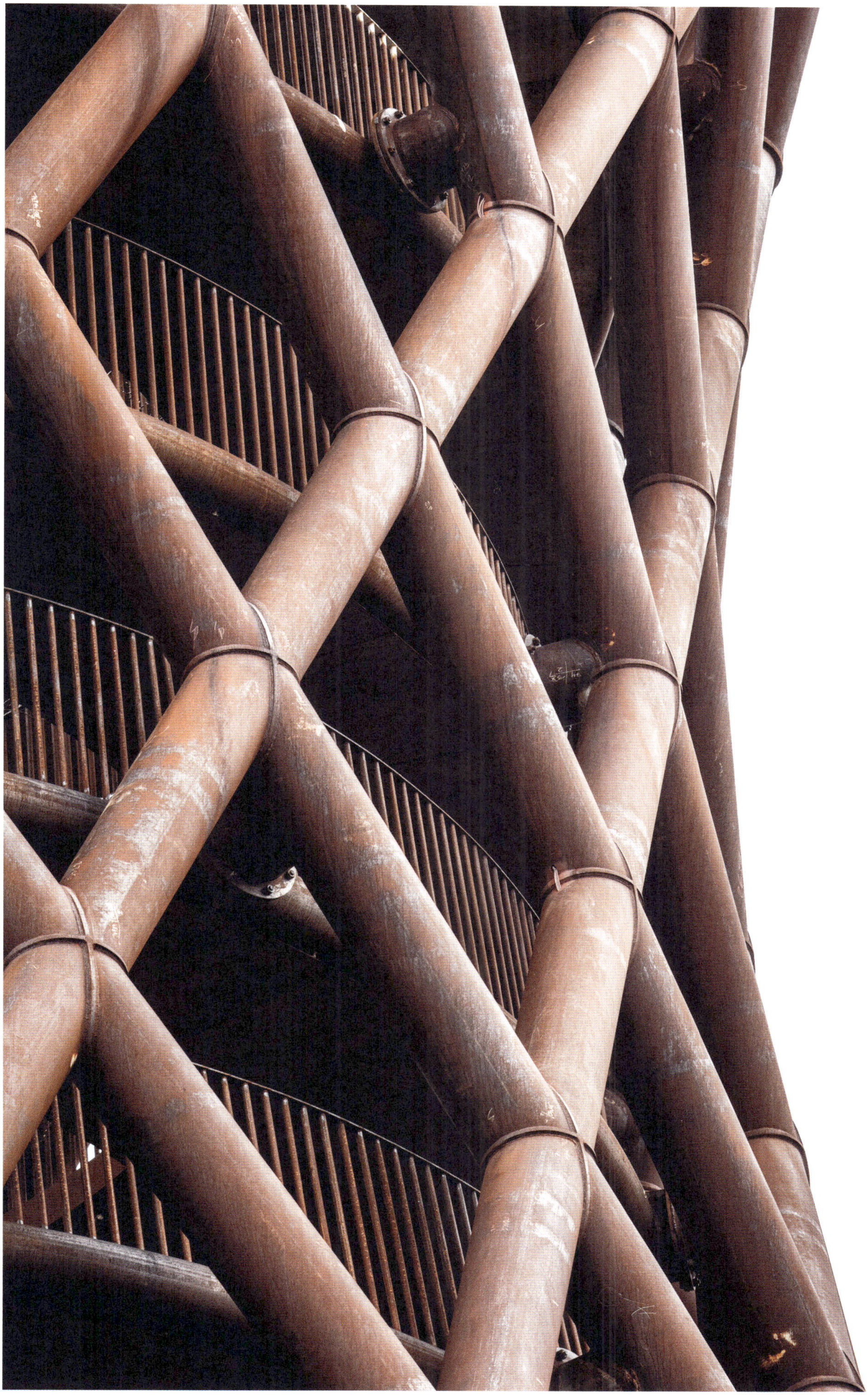

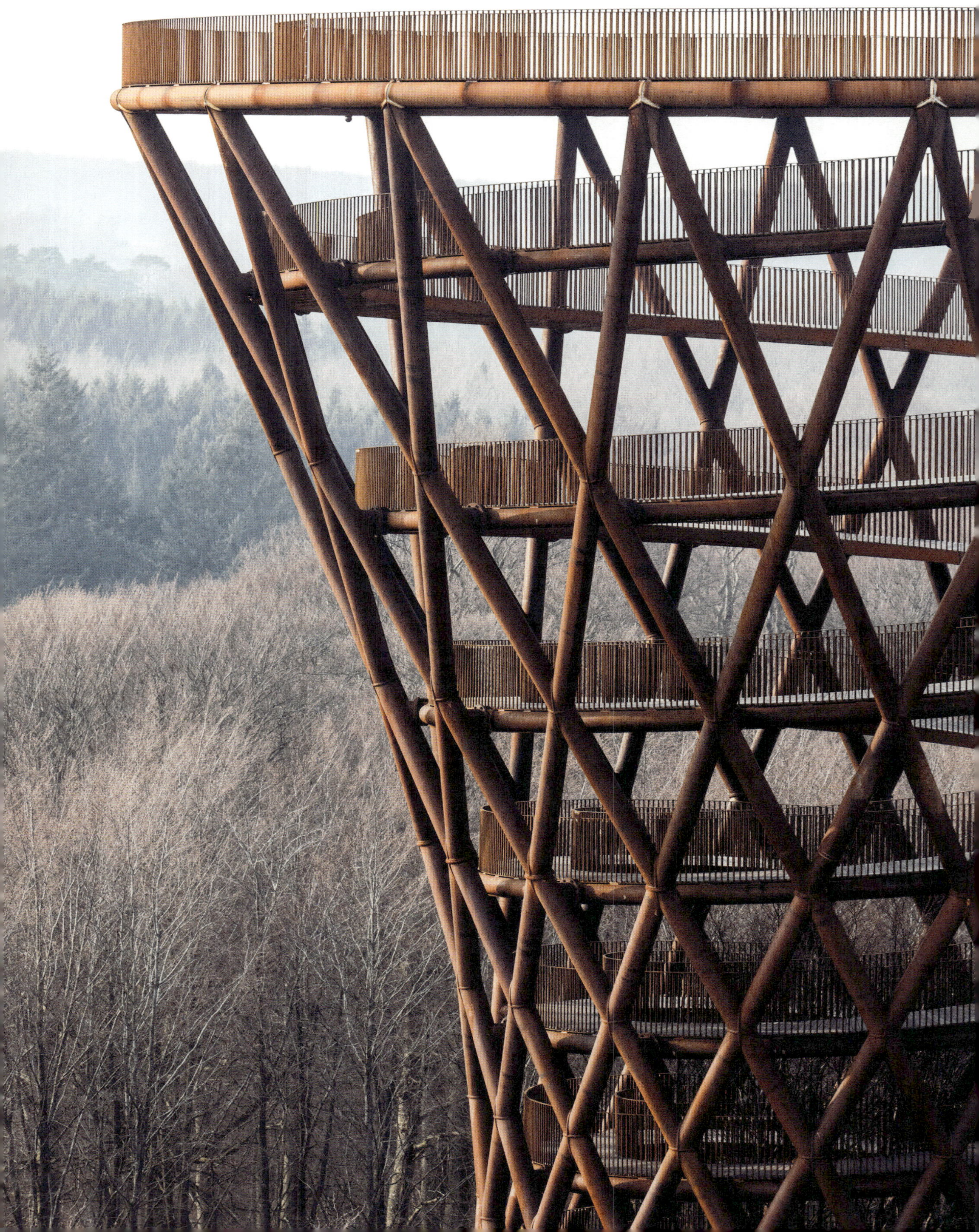

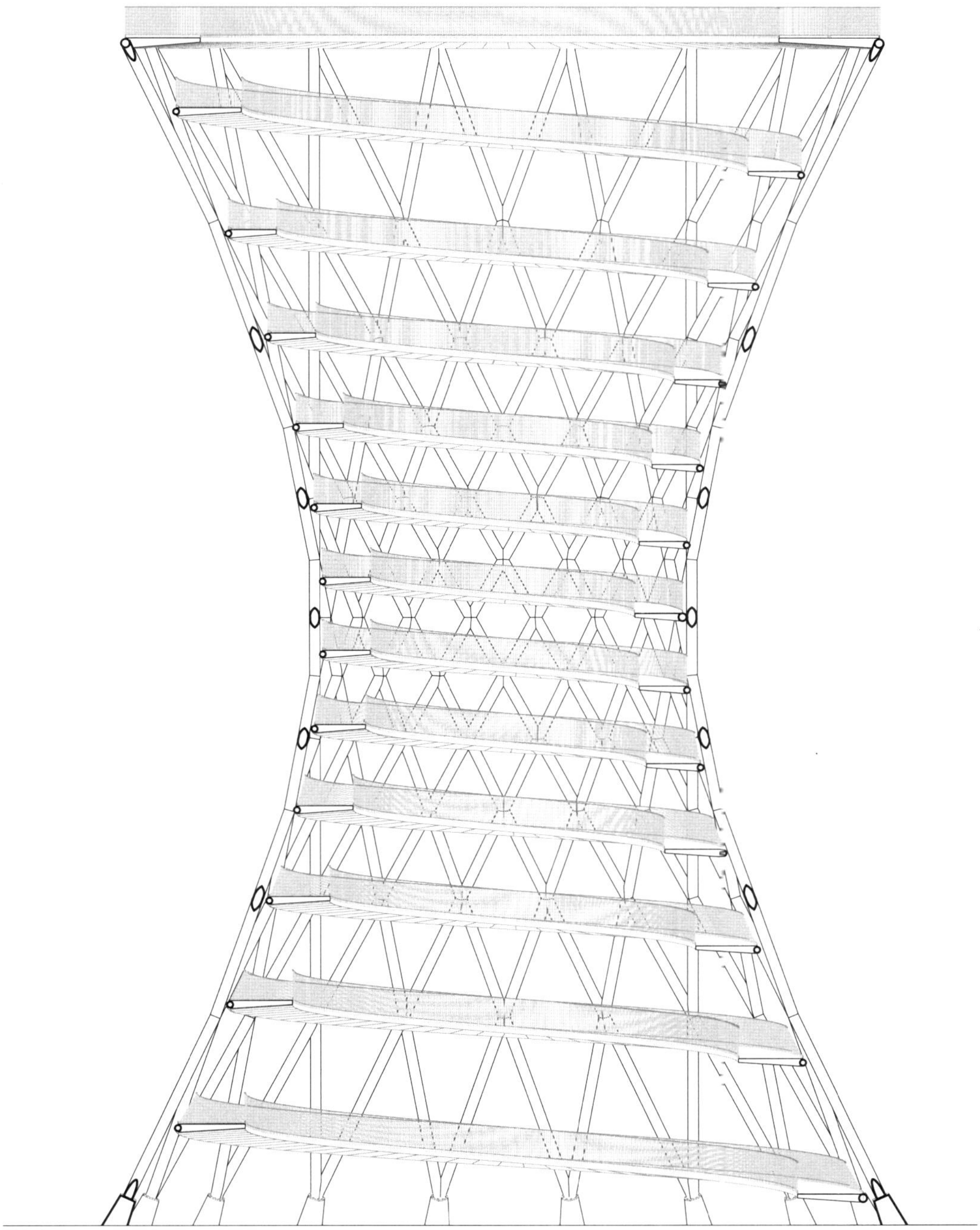

The spiralling ramp leads from ground level to the top
in one continuous movement.

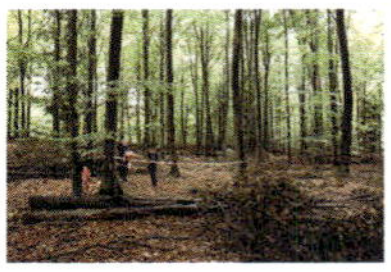

October

The specific site of the Forest Tower is selected, including the three trees in the middle of the tower

The site is selected: the Forest Tower will be built in a beautiful beech wood at a suitable distance from the old trees on the cliff west of the tower. Three tall, beautiful beech trees of uniform size and height, forming a harmonious triangle, are selected as the centre of the tower. Barrier tape is used to mark a perimeter around the three trees.

November

The soil analysis is planned

The Forest Tower is situated in the middle of a forest, which means that there is no soil data for the site. Moreover, all materials need to be driven across the uneven and, due to the season, wet forest floor to reach the site. The process of collecting soil samples is carefully planned.

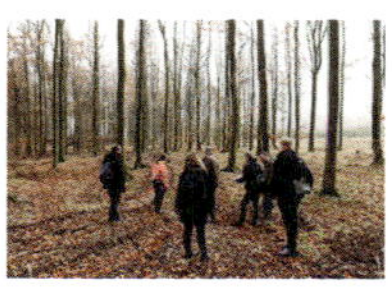

December

Faxe City Council passes detail plan

Faxe City Council unanimously passes the detail plan for the tower and the expansion of Camp Adventure. The plans for the expansion and, in particular, for the Forest Tower have enjoyed widespread support from Faxe Municipality throughout.

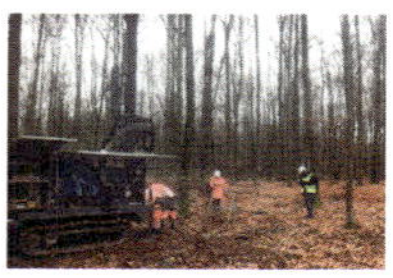

December

Soil sampling process begins

The 45-m-tall tower is situated 95 m above sea level on a ridge and will extend far above the treetops. The height, weight and wind impact necessitate a strong foundation. The calculations for the foundation are based on the soil samples, which are collected at 20 metres' depth in three different places on the intended site of the Forest Tower.

2017

June

The plans for the Forest Tower become the most-read story on the Danish newspaper Politiken's website

The initial renderings are distributed to the media, and the news of the tower at Camp Adventure spread to media all over the world. In Denmark, the news piece about the tower becomes the most-read story on the Danish newspaper Politiken's website two days in a row, 13 and 14 June 2017.

August

The Forest Tower wins an ICONIC AWARD in the Concept category

The tower wins first prize in the German Design Council's ICONIC AWARDS, the Concept category for not-yet-realized buildings. In particular, the jury highlights the visionary quality of the idea for the tower in the forest.

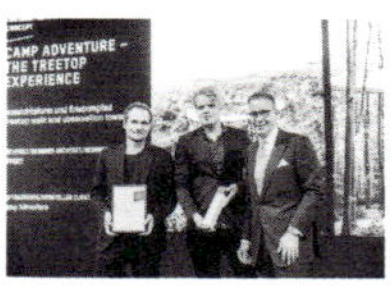

September

The route to and from the Forest Tower is planned

There are 900 m from the reception to the Forest Tower. The route to and from the Forest Tower is designed to go through different areas of the forest, across Brødebækken brook, and wind its way in among the trees. The route is marked with wooden stakes.

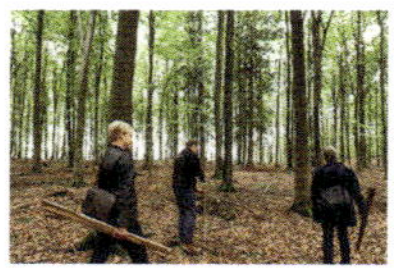

2018

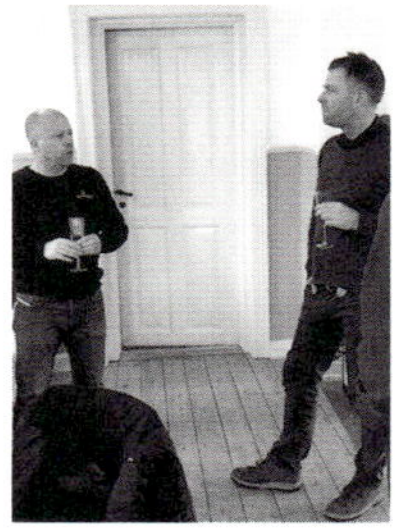

February

Levi Jensen and Stål & Design are commissioned as contractors

Camp Adventure signs a contract with Levi Jensen and Stål & Design to construct the tower. Both are local builders from the nearby towns of Herfølge and Næstved.

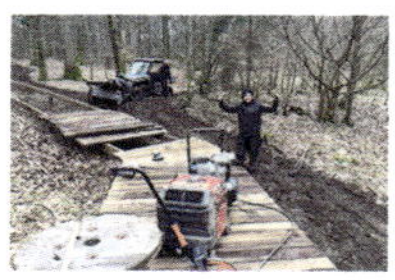

March

Construction of the boardwalk begins

Construction of the 1.8-km-long boardwalk on the forest floor begins. Concrete pillars are buried in the ground, girders are mounted on the concrete pillars, and, finally, planks are installed as the top layer.

May

Groundbreaking ceremony for the construction of the Forest Tower

The groundbreaking ceremony for the tower takes place on 3 May 2018 led by then Minister of Industry, Business and Financial Affairs, Brian Mikkelsen; Mayor of Faxe, Ole Vive; and Gisselfeld Kloster's CEO, Jens Risom. The ceremony marks the beginning of an unusual construction project in the middle of a wood. Throughout the construction period, many interested onlookers stop by the site every day.

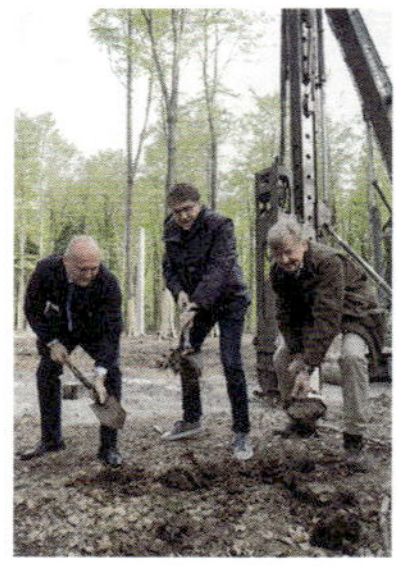

July

The foundation is constructed

The foundation is constructed from March to August. The foundation consists of 36 concrete pillars at a depth of 17–18 m. On top of the pillars is a 2-m-wide and 1-m-tall top ring. The top ring supports 18 truncated cones, which in turn will support the 36 steel tubes that form the exterior construction.

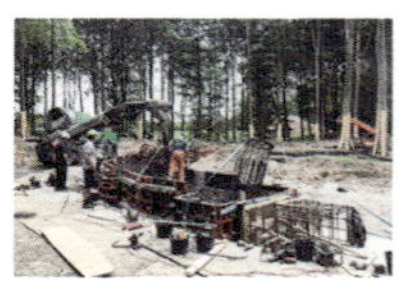

Timeline

2014

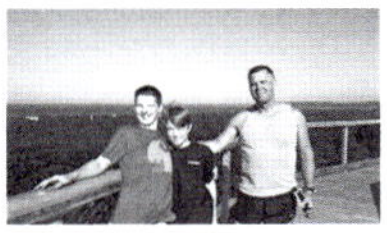

July

Field trip to the German island of Rügen

A small delegation from Camp Adventure visits the German island of Rügen to see the boardwalk and the tower at Naturerbe Zentrum Rügen. Impressed with the concept and tower, during their trip back to Denmark, they decide to pursue the idea of a tower in the woods near Camp Adventure.

December

Field trip to the German island of Rügen with the then Faxe Tourism Association

Camp Adventure invites the then Faxe Tourism Association and other local stakeholders on a trip to Naturerbe Zentrum Rügen to be introduced to the envisioned attraction at Camp Adventure.

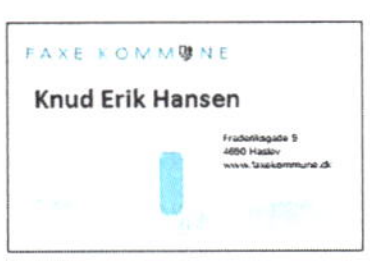

September

First meeting with Faxe Municipality

Visions and ambitions are presented to Faxe Municipality, with a focus on the potential effect of a tower on Camp Adventure as well as on Faxe Municipality and southern Zealand in general. As part of the presentation, a big, iconic tower has been added to the then mayor's business card.

2015

March

EFFEKT Architects is commissioned to design the Forest Tower

EFFEKT Architects is commissioned to develop the concept for the tower in cooperation with Camp Adventure. EFFEKT is a Danish architecture and urban design firm with projects all over the world.

July

Rambøll is commissioned to prepare a municipal detail plan and an EPA

Realizing the vision of a tower at Camp Adventure requires many official permits. Rambøll is commissioned to prepare a municipal detail plan and an EPA (environmental impact assessment) for the entire area in cooperation with Camp Adventure. Rambøll is one of Denmark's biggest consultancy firms with extensive expertise in construction, transport and environment, among other areas.

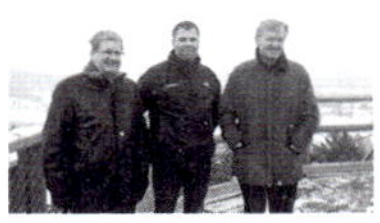

March

Field trip to Neuschönau in Germany with Faxe Municipality and Gisselfeld Kloster

Together with Faxe Municipality and Gisselfeld Kloster, Camp Adventure goes on a field trip to Neuschönau, Germany, to see the first forest tower built in Germany: Treetop Walk Bavarian Forest. The impressions from this trip convince Faxe Municipality and Gisselfeld Kloster to support a tower at Camp Adventure.

October

Field trip to Neuschönau, Germany, with EFFEKT Architects

Camp Adventure and EFFEKT go on a field trip to Treetop Walk Bavarian Forest to form an impression of the German tower and begin to define the visual expression of the tower at Camp Adventure. The trip to Germany inspires the desire to have a large platform as the culmination of the climb inside the tower and to bring the visitors closer to the interior trees.

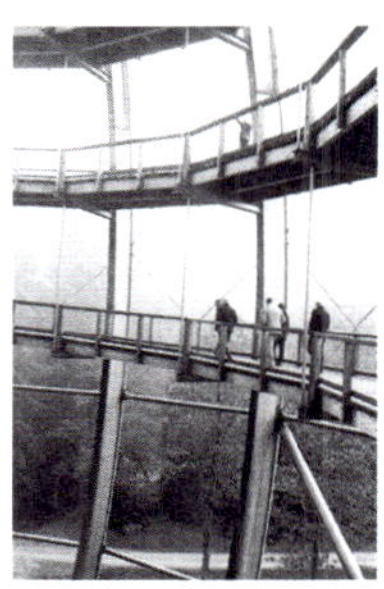

2016

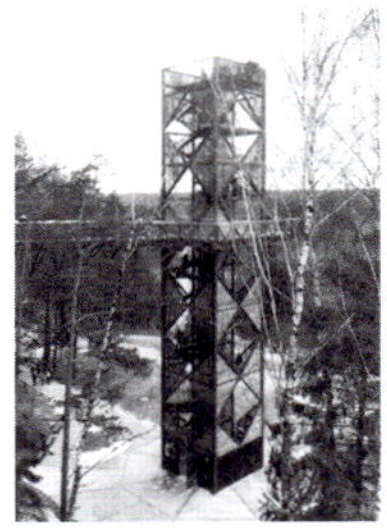

March

Field trip til Anykščiai, Lithuania

Camp Adventure goes on a field trip to the tower in Anykščiai, Lithuania. Among other input, the trip provides inspiration to the idea of building the Camp Adventure tower in steel rather than wood as originally intended.

July

The Danish Agency for Water and Nature Management grants exemption from The Forestry Act

Camp Adventure is situated in a wood that is subject to the Danish protection of forest land against change in land use (Danish: *fredskov*). Nevertheless, the then Danish Agency for Water and Nature Management grants a rare exemption from The Forestry Act that allows for the construction of a tower in the Camp Adventure wood. Faxe Municipality, Gisselfeld Kloster and Camp Adventure celebrate the important milestone.

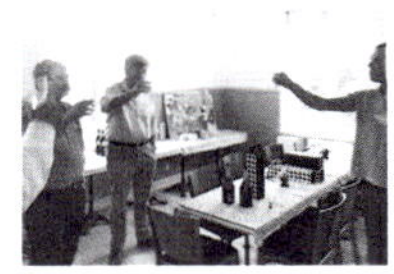

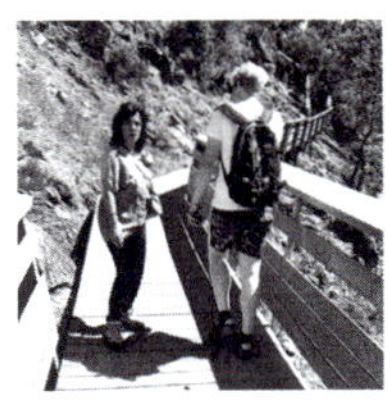

June

Field trip to Paiva, Portugal

A delegation from Camp Adventure visits Paiva Walkways in Arouca, Portugal, to look at the boardwalk along Paiva River. The 8-km-long, low boardwalk along the river provides the inspiration for a low boardwalk from the reception area to the tower and back again.

September

Arup is commissioned to carry out the engineering project

Arup is commissioned to carry out all the engineering work on the hourglass-shaped tower. Arup is one of the world's leading engineering firms and has been involved in such high-profile projects as the Øresund Bridge, the Chinese National Stadium for the Beijing Olympics and the Sydney Opera House.

October

From wood to steel

The architects decide to make the tower in corten steel, rather than wood, as initially suggested. Corten steel is maintenance-free, and the reddish-brown colour is a beautiful match for the colours of the forest.

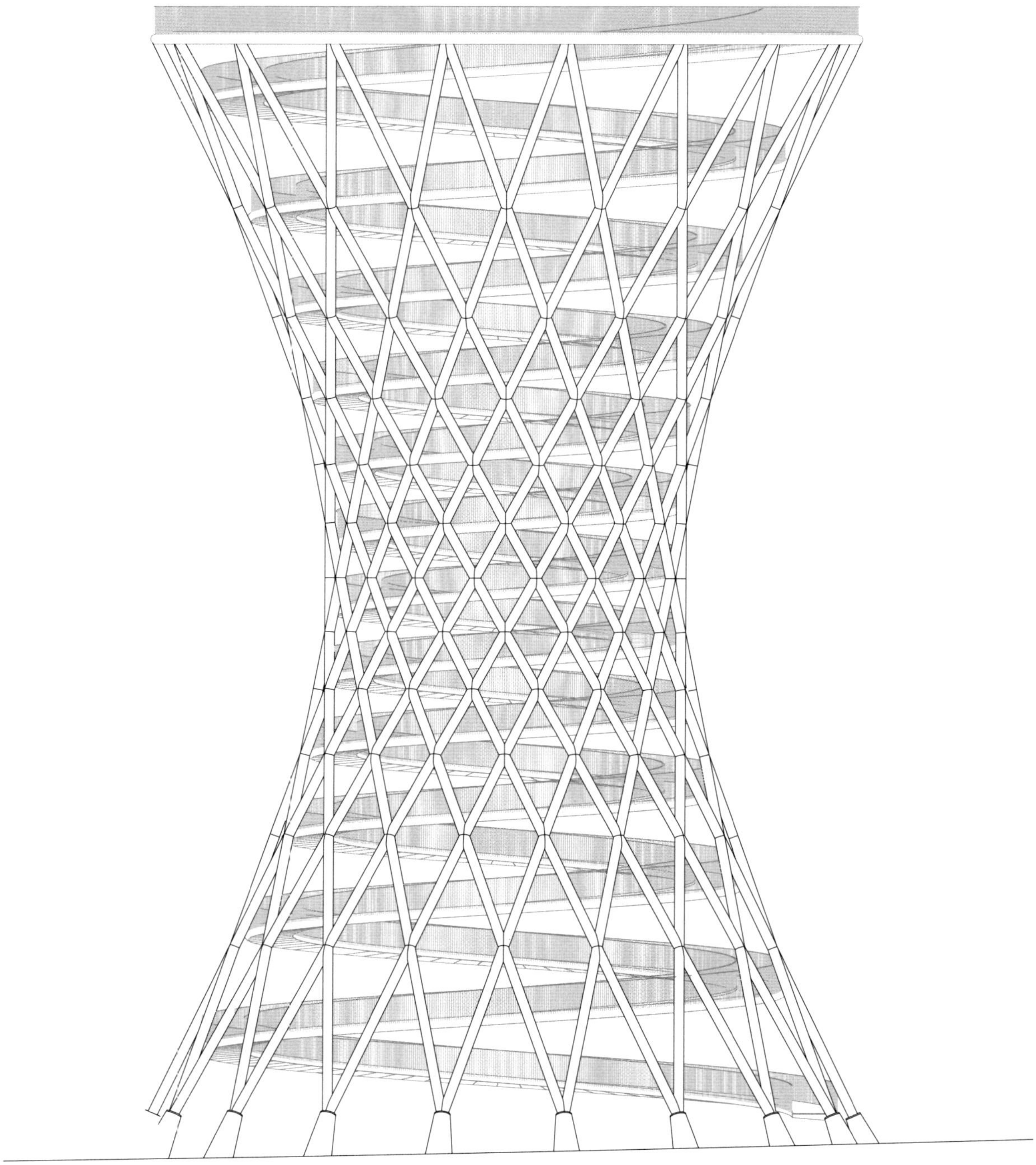

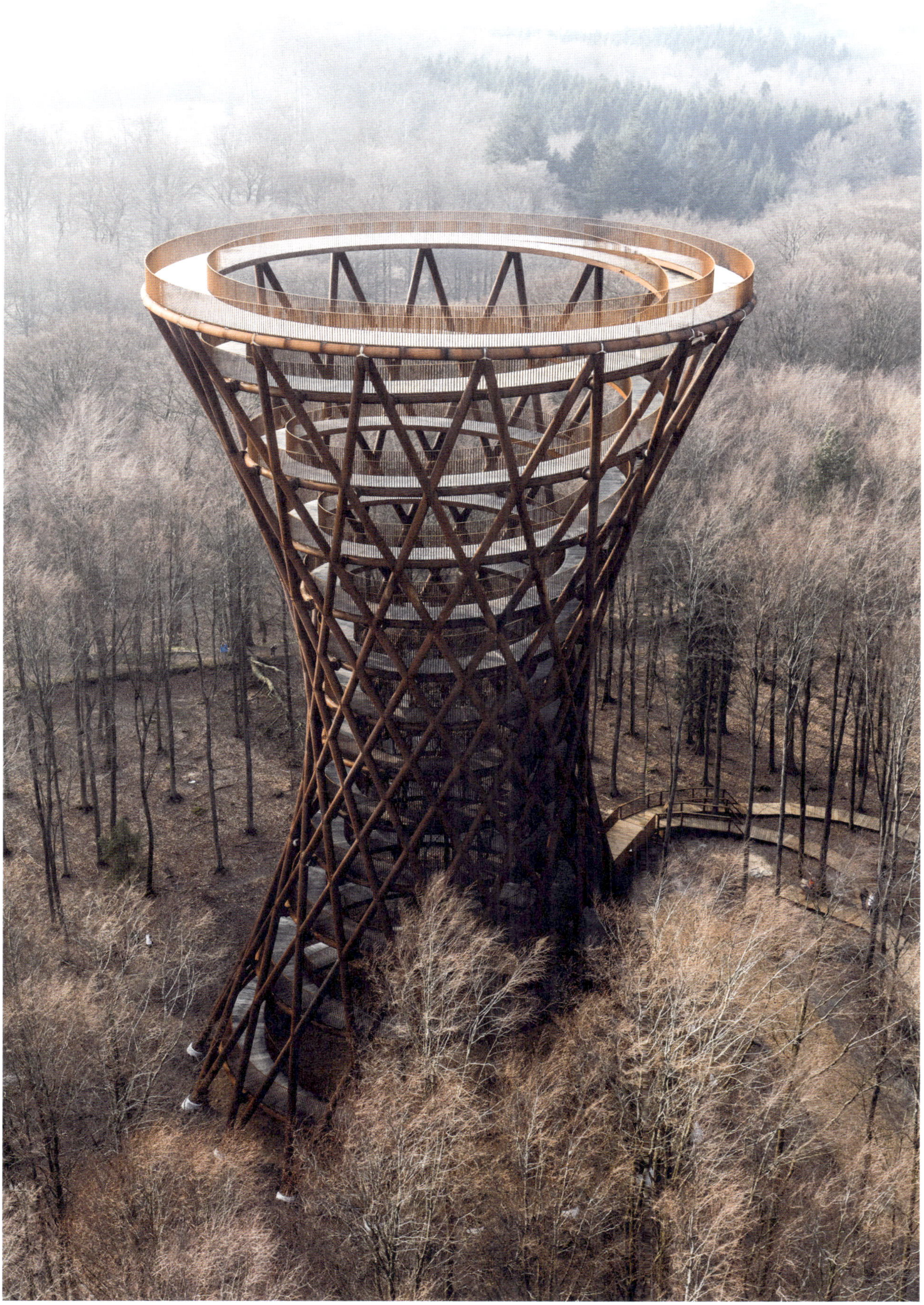

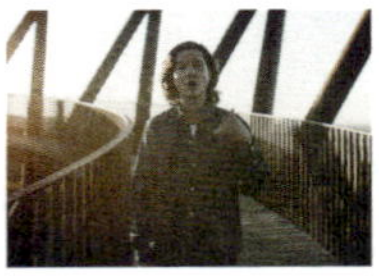

August

Lukas Graham shoots a music video at the Forest Tower

The Forest Tower is one of the settings in Lukas Graham's music video for the single 'Lie'. In September, the music video is released on YouTube, and by July 2020, it has been shown 12 million times.

September

The fund-raiser 'Danmark planter træer' (Denmark Plants Trees) raises DKK 20 million, enough to plant one million trees

Live on the Danish TV station TV2, the Forest Tower is the setting for the first Danish fund-raising show for tree planting. In total, the event raises DKK 20 million, enough to plant one million trees.

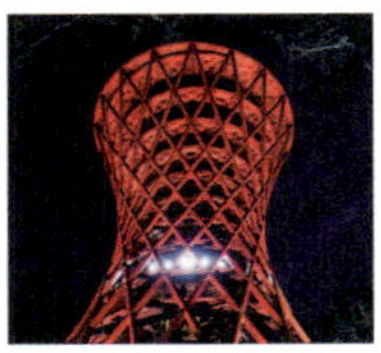

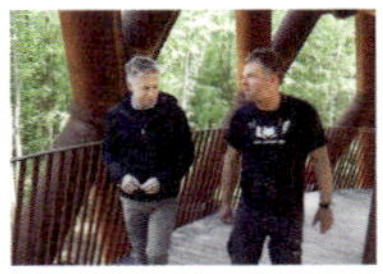

October

The Forest Tower is featured on CBS Sunday Morning, the most watched morning TV show in the United States

The American TV station CBS brings a story about the Forest Tower. By now, the Forest Tower has been featured in countless international media, but American media in particular take an interest in Camp Adventure, and Americans are the fourth biggest category of visitors to the Forest Tower.

December

Camp Adventure reaches 351,895 visitors

At the end of the first year, the total tally for Camp Adventure is 351,895 visitors from 74 countries. That puts Camp Adventure into the Top 25 of Danish attractions on the tourism association Visit Denmark's list for 2018 and makes it the most-visited attraction on the island of Zealand outside Greater Copenhagen.

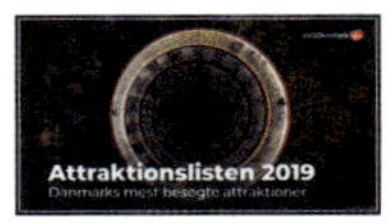

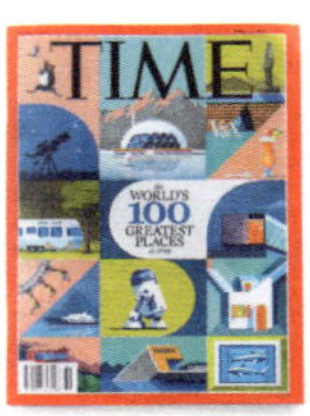

September

TIME Magazine includes the Forest Tower on its list of the World's Greatest 100 Places

The leading American medium TIME Magazine includes the Forest Tower as one of the World's 100 Greatest Places to visit in 2019. The Forest Tower is the only Danish attraction on the prestigious list that year. The previous year, three Danish attractions were included: the Tivoli Gardens, the Experimentarium and the Noma restaurant. Camp Adventure has rapidly become a world-class attraction.

September

Camp Adventure reaches 300,000 visitors in 2019

In September, the camp welcomes its visitor no. 300,000. After the Danish summer holidays, most of the visitors to the Forest Tower are tourists from abroad.

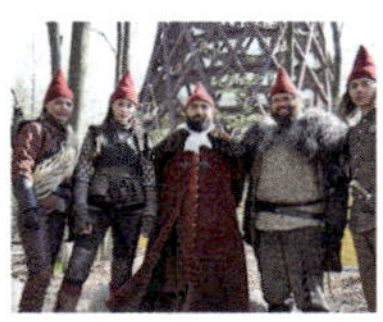

December

The Forest Tower is one of the settings of TV 2's advent calendar show 'Tinka & Kongespillet'

No fewer than 1.3 million viewers tune in for the two episodes of TV2's Christmas advent series 'Tinka & Kongespillet' that are filmed at the Forest Tower. In the series, the Forest Tower features as *Himmeltårnet* (Sky Tower) and is part of the elf kingdom.

2020

May

400,000 visitors

Since the opening of the Forest Tower, Camp Adventure has now had a total of 400,000 visitors.

July

500,000 visitors

During the busy month of July, the total number of visitors to Camp Adventure since the opening of the Forest Tower passes the half-million mark.

August

600,000 visitors

The year 2020 looks set to become another successful year for Camp Adventure, as guest number 600,000 visits the adventure site in August.

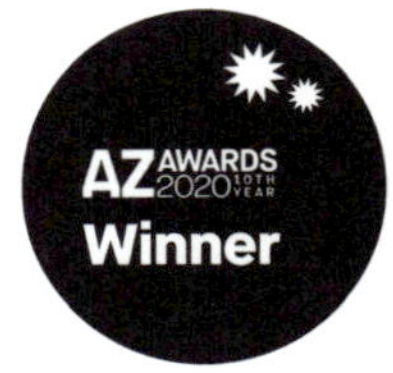

September

Winner of AZURE Magazine's AZ Awards 2020

In the AZ Awards 2020, the Forest Tower makes a clean sweep in the 'Landscape Architecture' category, winning both the jury's award and the AZURE Magazine's readership vote.

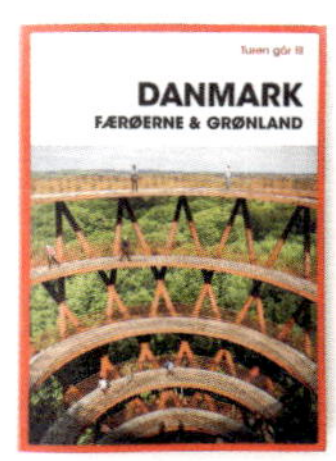

August

Turen går til

Turen går til ... is a renowned series of travel guides that has been showing tourists around Denmark and the rest of the world since 1952. This year, the iconic book cover features an equally iconic destination: the Forest Tower.

September

The view from the tower is in jeopardy

In the neighbouring municipality of Næstved, plans have been underway to build three 150-metre-tall wind turbines about 1.5 km from the Forest Tower. Faxe Municipality, where the Forest Tower is located, files a formal complaint, as the giant structures would interfere with the view from the tower. Minister of Industry, Business and Financial Affairs Simon Kollerup has the last say in the matter. Ultimately, Camp Adventure and Faxe Municipality prevail, and the Forest Tower retains its spectacular view without the interference of giant wind turbines.

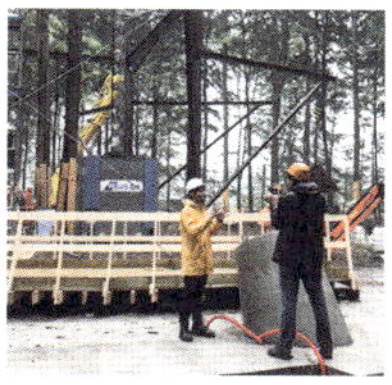

September

Der Spiegel shoots a video from the building site

Many news media outlets visit the construction site, including the biggest German-language medium, Der Spiegel, which posts a video on their website. The French newspaper Le Figaro also reports on the project.

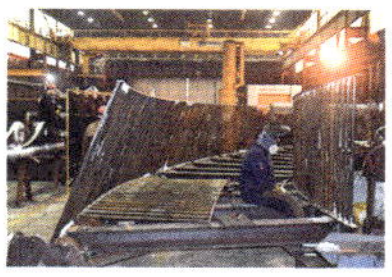

October

The railing is installed on the ramp elements

The 1.2-m-tall railing is delivered in separate sections, which are installed on the interior and exterior sides of the ramp. The installation of the railing takes place on the same location where the joists and oak planks are being installed on the ramp sections.

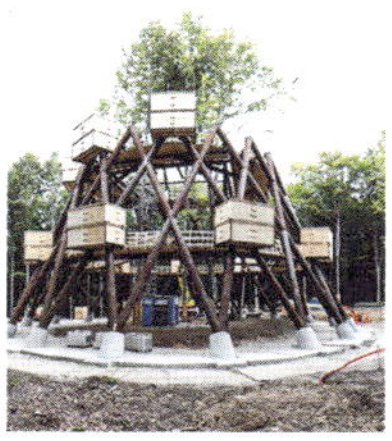

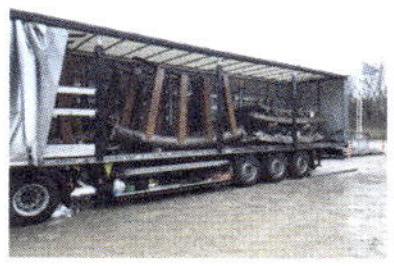

December

Wood is installed on the ramp elements

The spiral-shaped ramp consists of 165 steel sections. In total, there are 22 different kinds of ramp sections, each 4–5 m long. The steel plant delivers them bare to another factory, where joists and planks are installed before they are transported to the construction site.

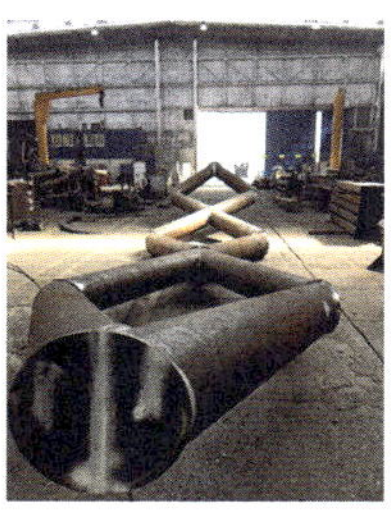

September

Mounting of diagrid

The 54 diagrid construction parts are prefabricated in a workshop and then transported to the site for assembly.

November

Construction is in full swing

From August 2018 to March 2019, the Forest Tower itself is constructed. The Forest Tower is built in three sections, each 15 m tall. Each section has 18 prefab steel elements, which are transported to the construction site and then welded together. Much of the welding work takes place in wooden cabins attached to the outside of the tower, where the welders are sheltered from the wind and rain. A temporary interior tower stabilizes the elements and serves as scaffolding for the workers. Once the entire outer structure is finished, a top ring is added. Now, the tower has attained structural integrity on its own, and the temporary tower is dismantled. Next, the 165 internal steel sections clad with wooden planks are installed and welded into place to form the spiral ramp.

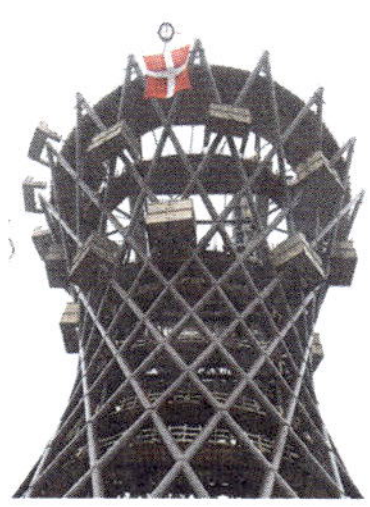

December

Topping off at the Forest Tower

On 20 December 2018, just before the Christmas holidays, it is time for topping off. The ceremony marks that the construction has now reached full height, and true to tradition, the Danish flag and a wreath are mounted at the top of the structure. The tower is now visible from afar, high above the tree crowns.

2019

January

A tower in a tower

During the construction phase, there is a temporary tower inside the Forest Tower. The temporary structure stabilizes the external steel sections and also serves as a working platform for the builders. Like the Forest Tower itself, the temporary tower is built in three sections, and before construction can begin on a new section of the Forest Tower, the builders first have to construct the matching section of the temporary tower. Thus, the project in fact involves the construction of two towers in the middle of the forest. The top section of the temporary tower is removed from the outside, using ropes.

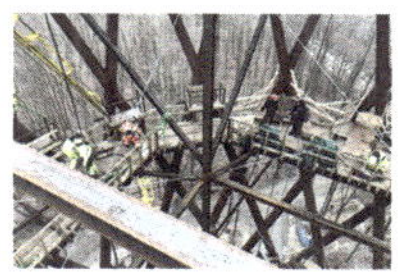

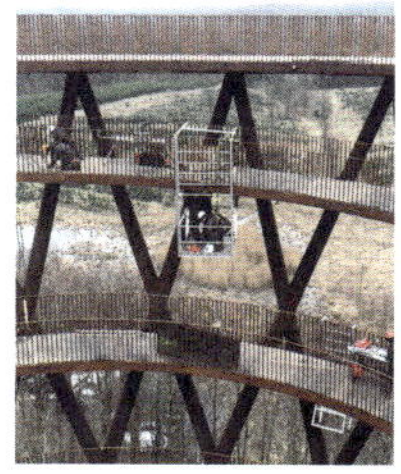

March

Face plates are screwed onto the ramp

Face plates are mounted on the underside of the ramp to form a uniform, closed 'ceiling' from the base of the Forest Tower to the top. The face plates are thin corten steel sheets, and their purpose is strictly aesthetic.

March

Official opening of the Forest Tower

Then Prime Minister Lars Løkke Rasmussen opens the tower on Saturday, 30 March. On this occasion, the tower is also officially named *Skovtårnet*, in English: the Forest Tower. Construction has taken a little under 11 months, and some 300 invited guests celebrate the event on a beautiful, sunny day.

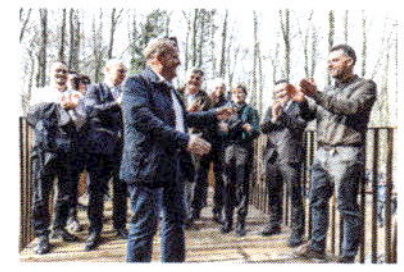

March

The Forest Tower opens to the public

On Sunday, 31 March, the Forest Tower opens to the public – 130 years to the day after the opening of the Eiffel Tower. A large number of people show up on opening day and during Easter, which follows soon after.

March

The bridge over the brook is where the experience begins

From the reception area, the walk to the Forest Tower begins as one crosses the bridge over the winding brook Brødebæk, which runs through the entire Camp Adventure area. The bridge is about 20 m long and raised 5 m above the stream. Although this is where the experience begins, it is one of the last pieces to be finished. It is not ready until two days before the opening.

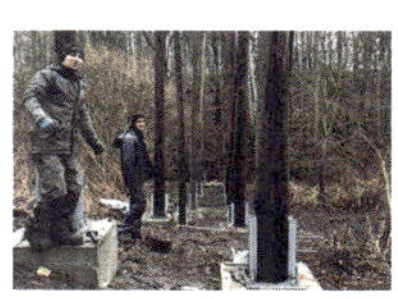

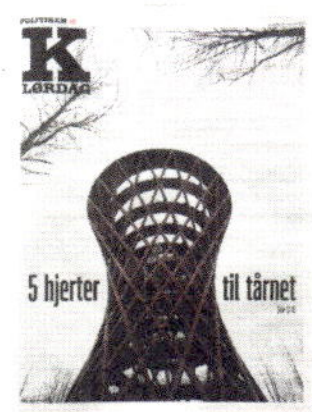

March

Politiken awards the tower five hearts out of six

Just before the official opening, a review in the Danish newspaper Politiken awards the tower five hearts out of six. The critic calls it 'an elegant blast!' and also writes 'the experience is intoxicating. But it also offers time for reflection during the long ascent towards the sky.'

June

Camp Adventure reaches 100,000 visitors in 2019

The Forest Tower has become a virtual tourist magnet, attracting visitors from near and far. In June, the site welcomes its visitor number 100,000 that year.

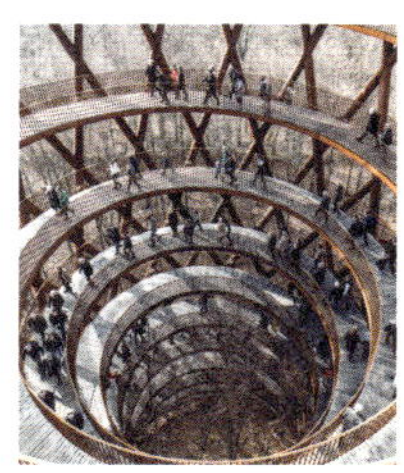

July

Camp Adventure reaches 200,000 visitors in 2019

In July alone, there are 70,000 visitors, and over the course of July, the total count for 2019 surpasses 200,000.

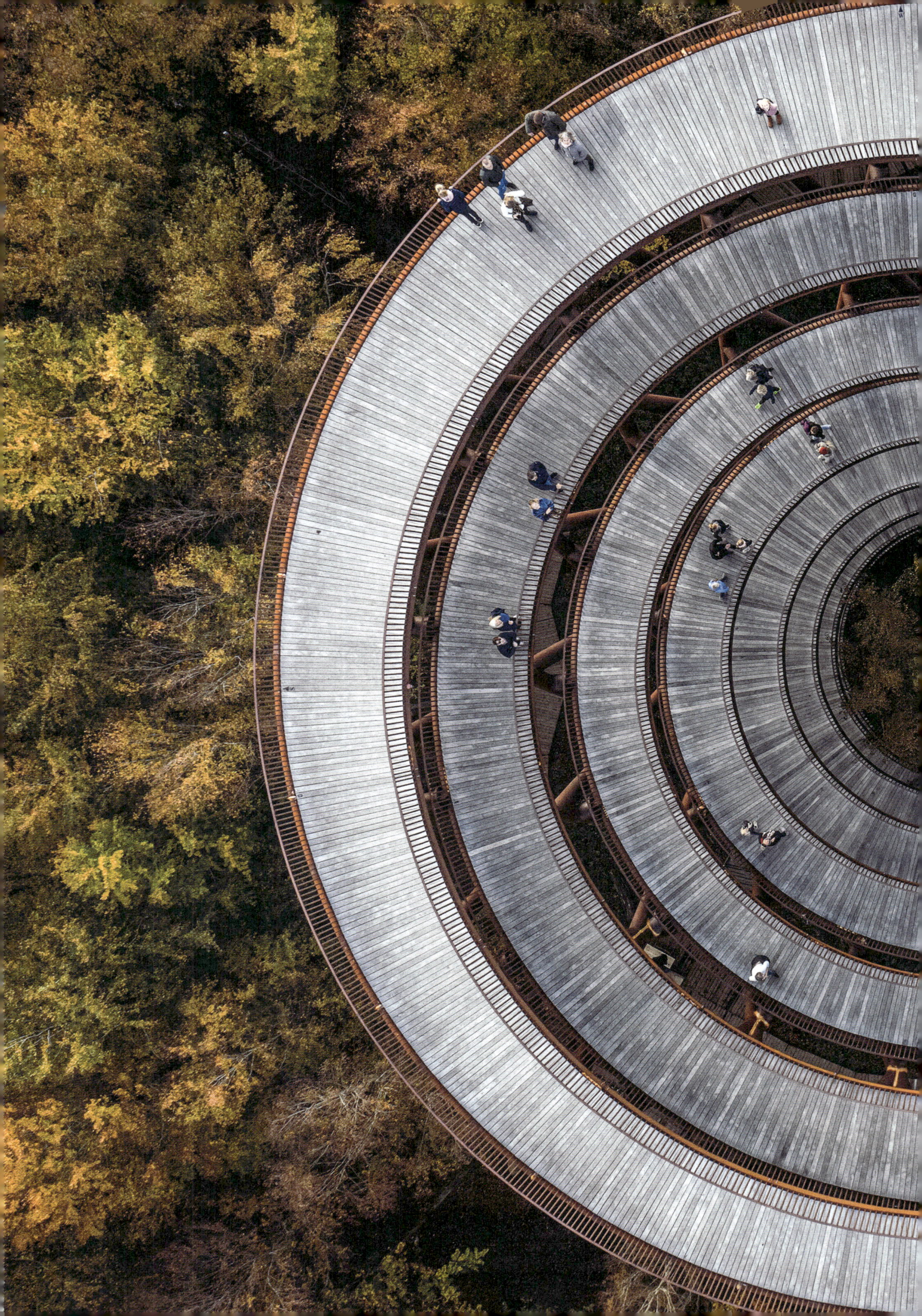

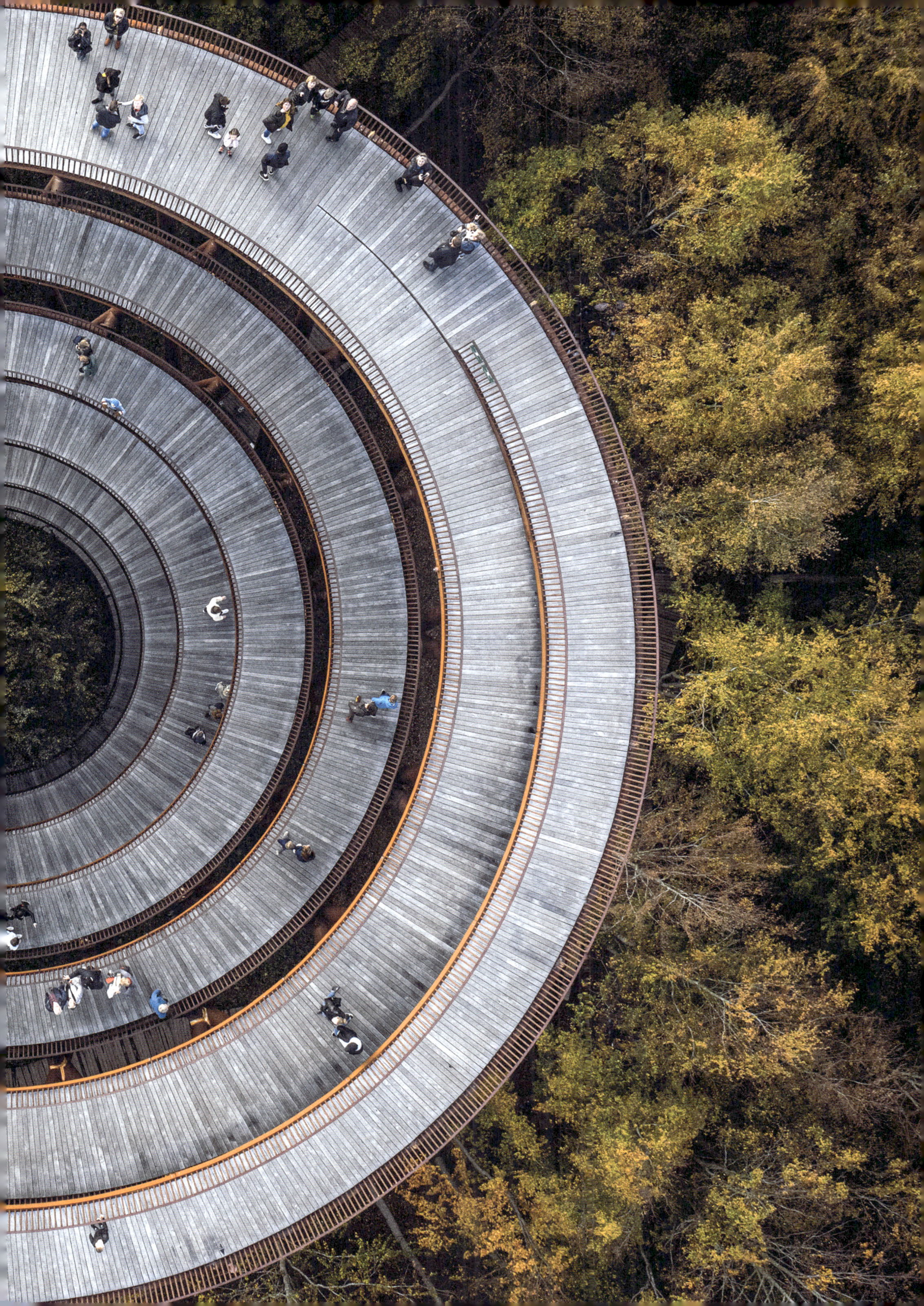

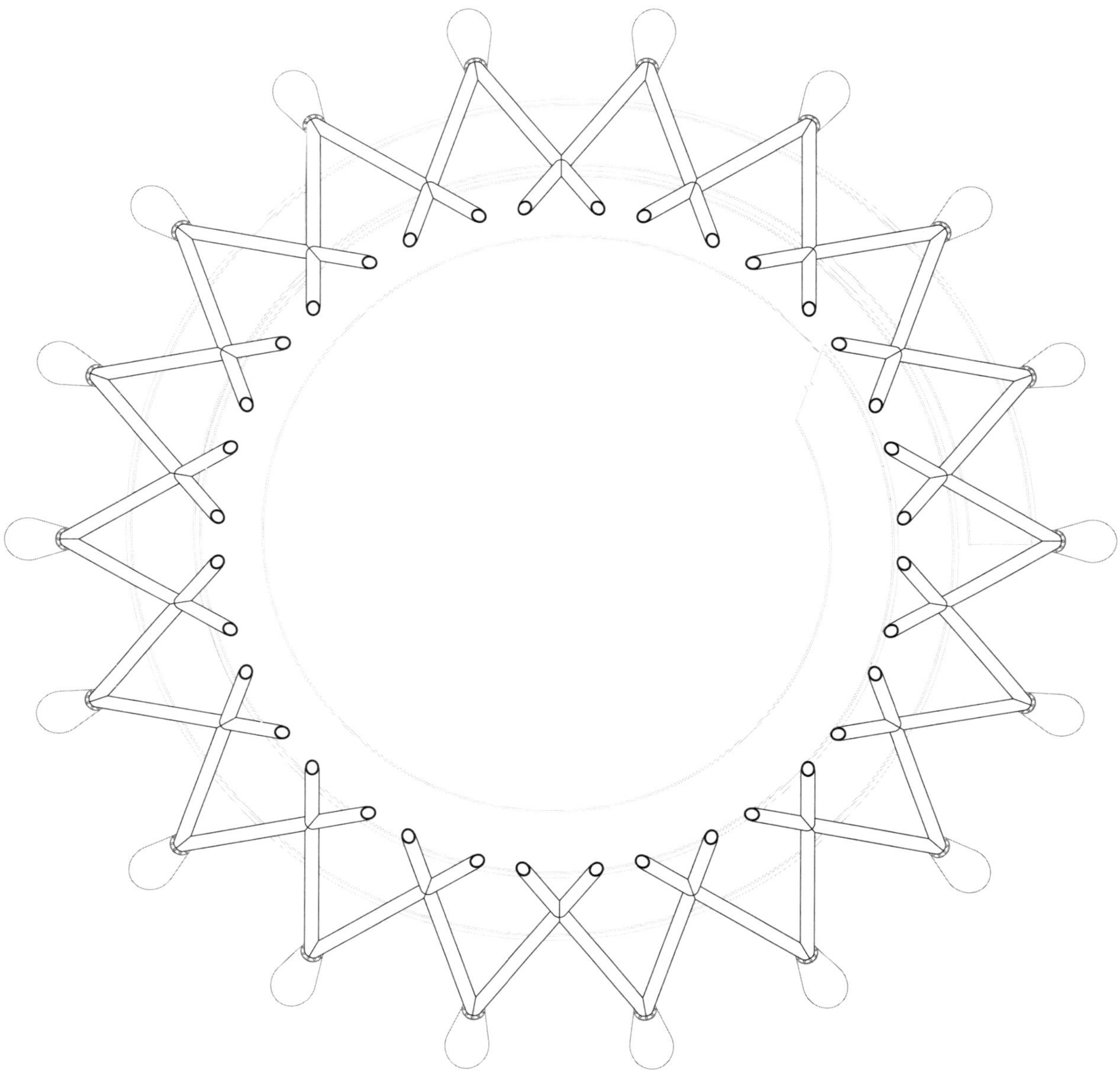

The hyperboloid shape results in a continuous variation in diameter, a dynamic aspect that makes the ascent inside the tower a fascinating experience.

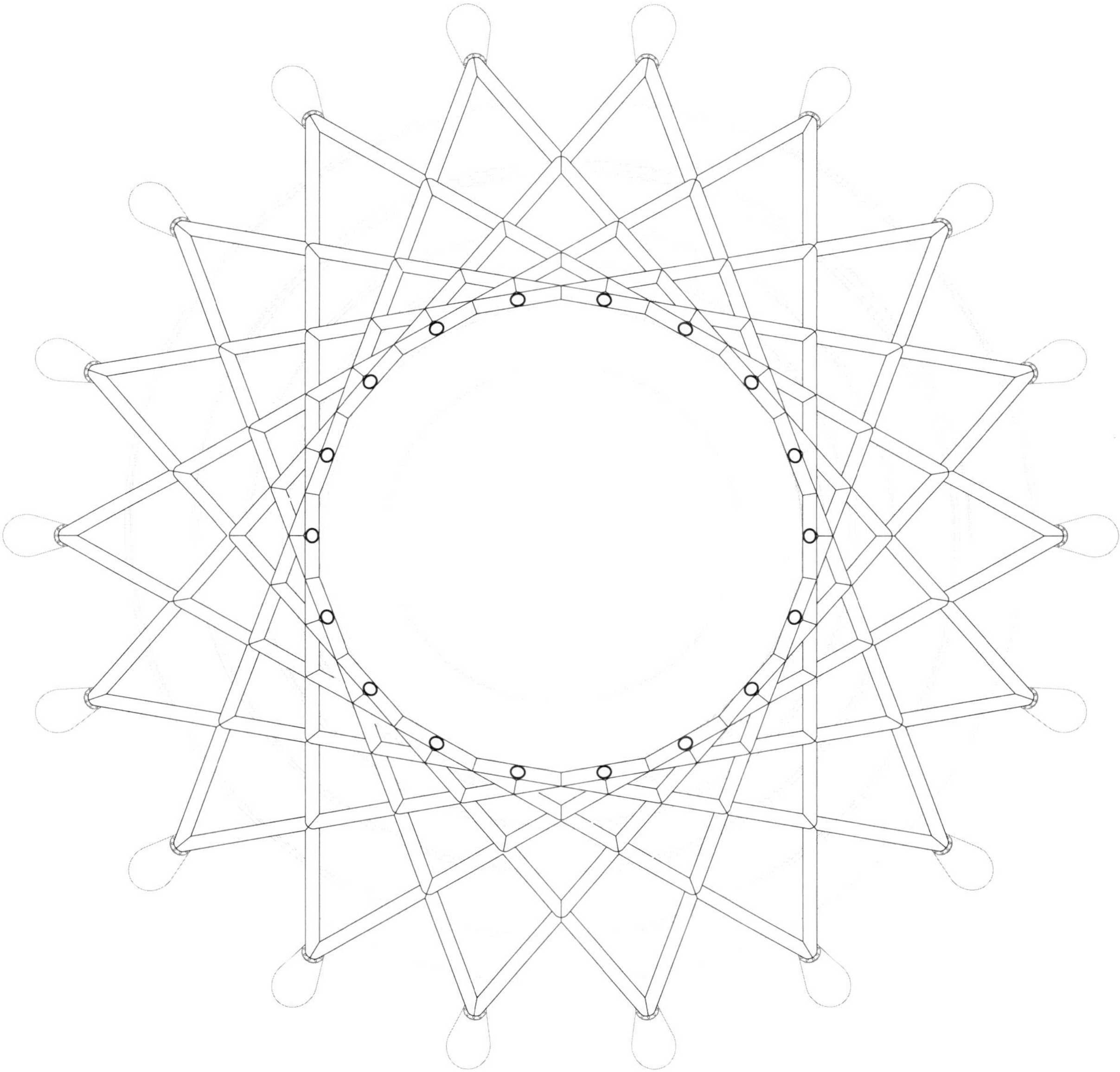

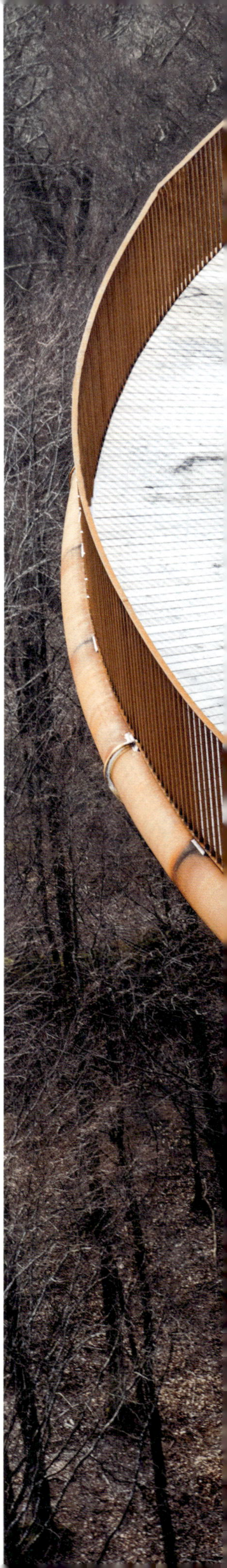

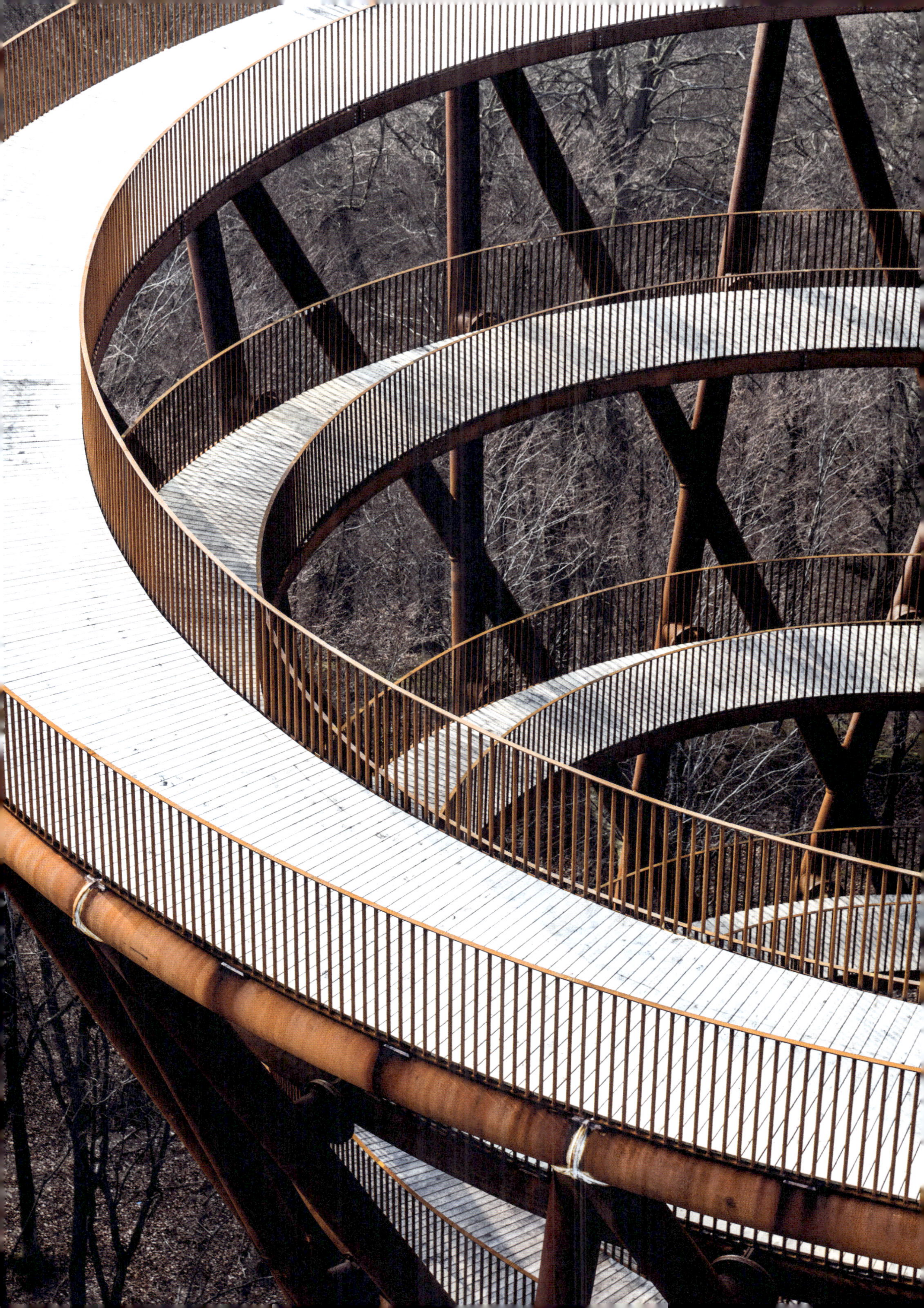

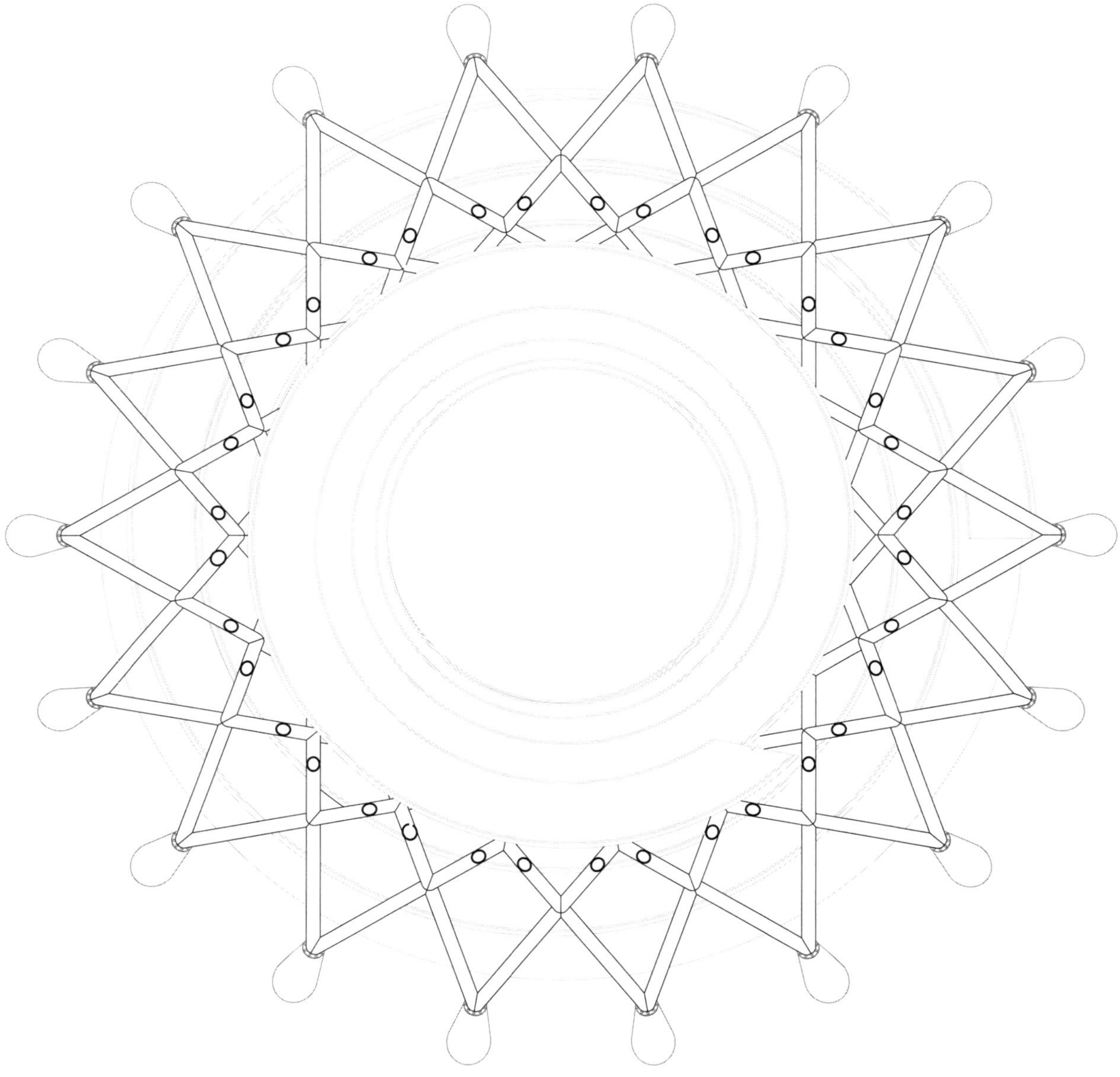

The ramp seamlessly transitions into the platform, which offers a panoramic 360-degree view.

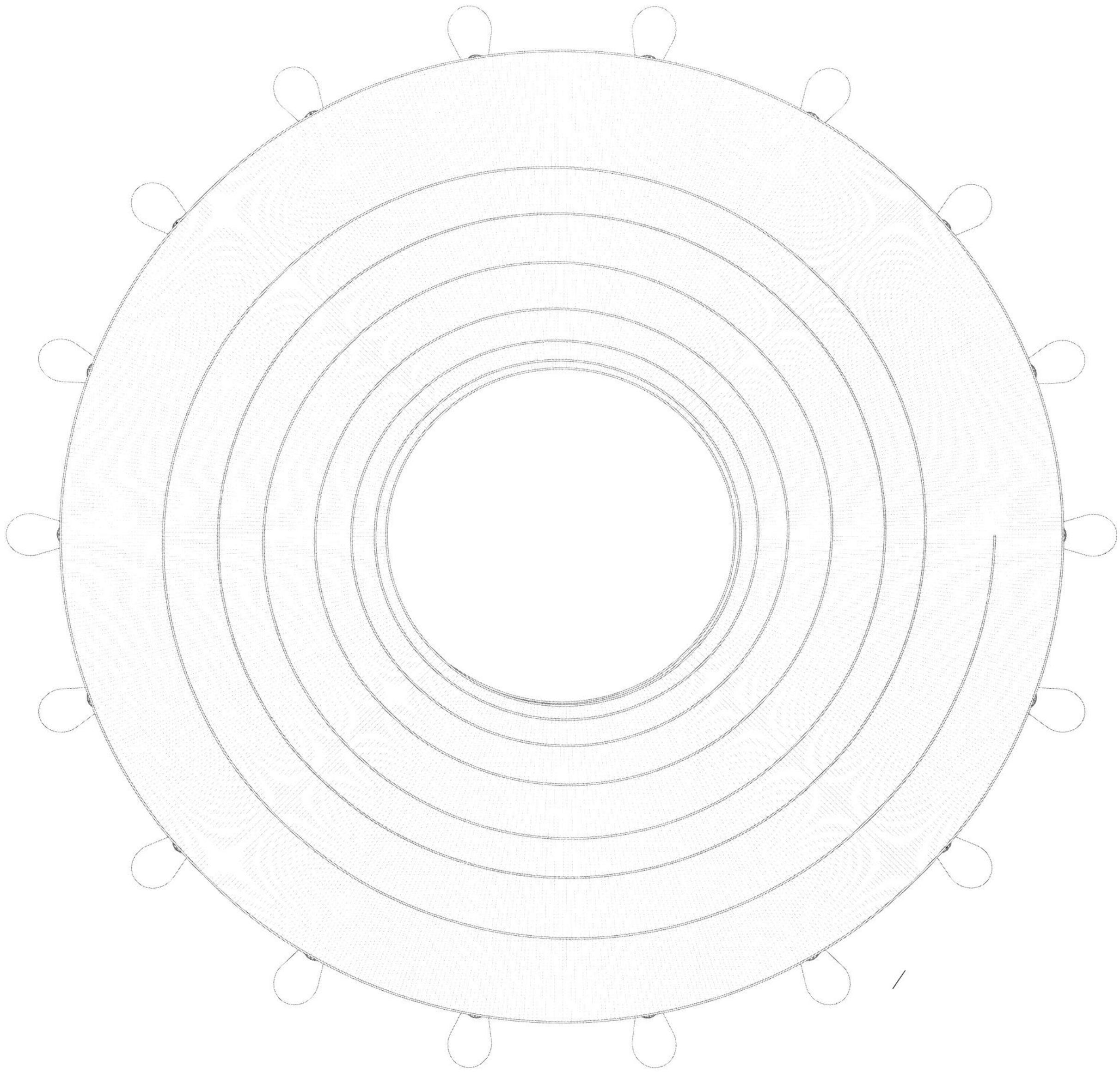

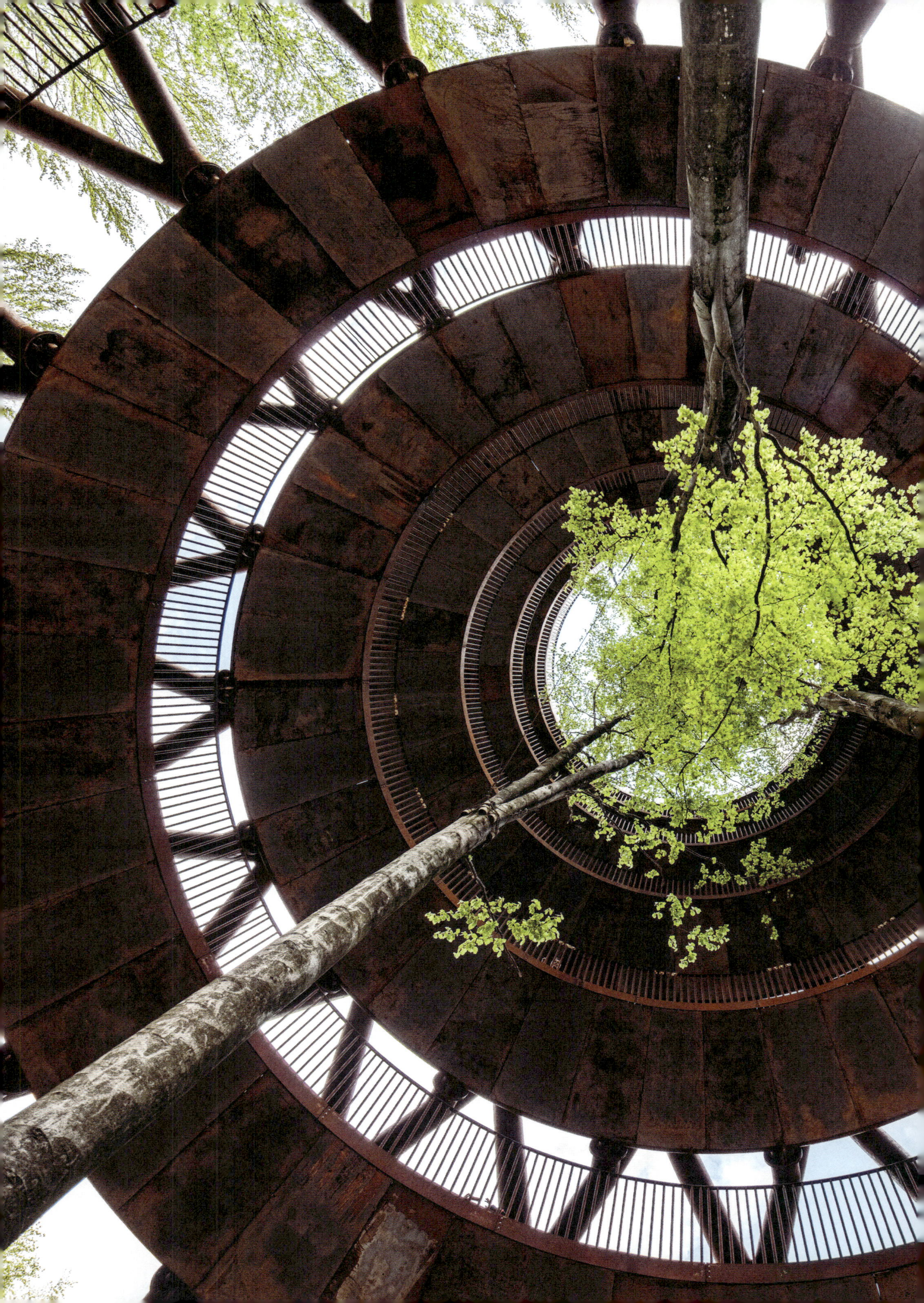

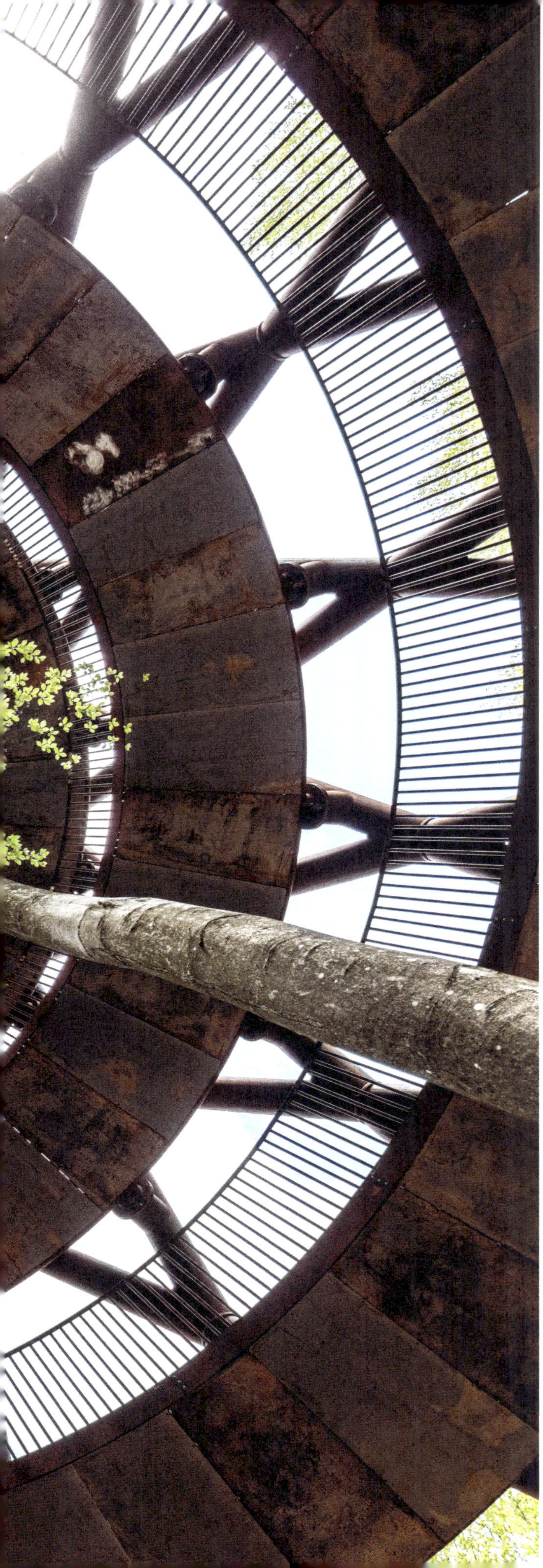

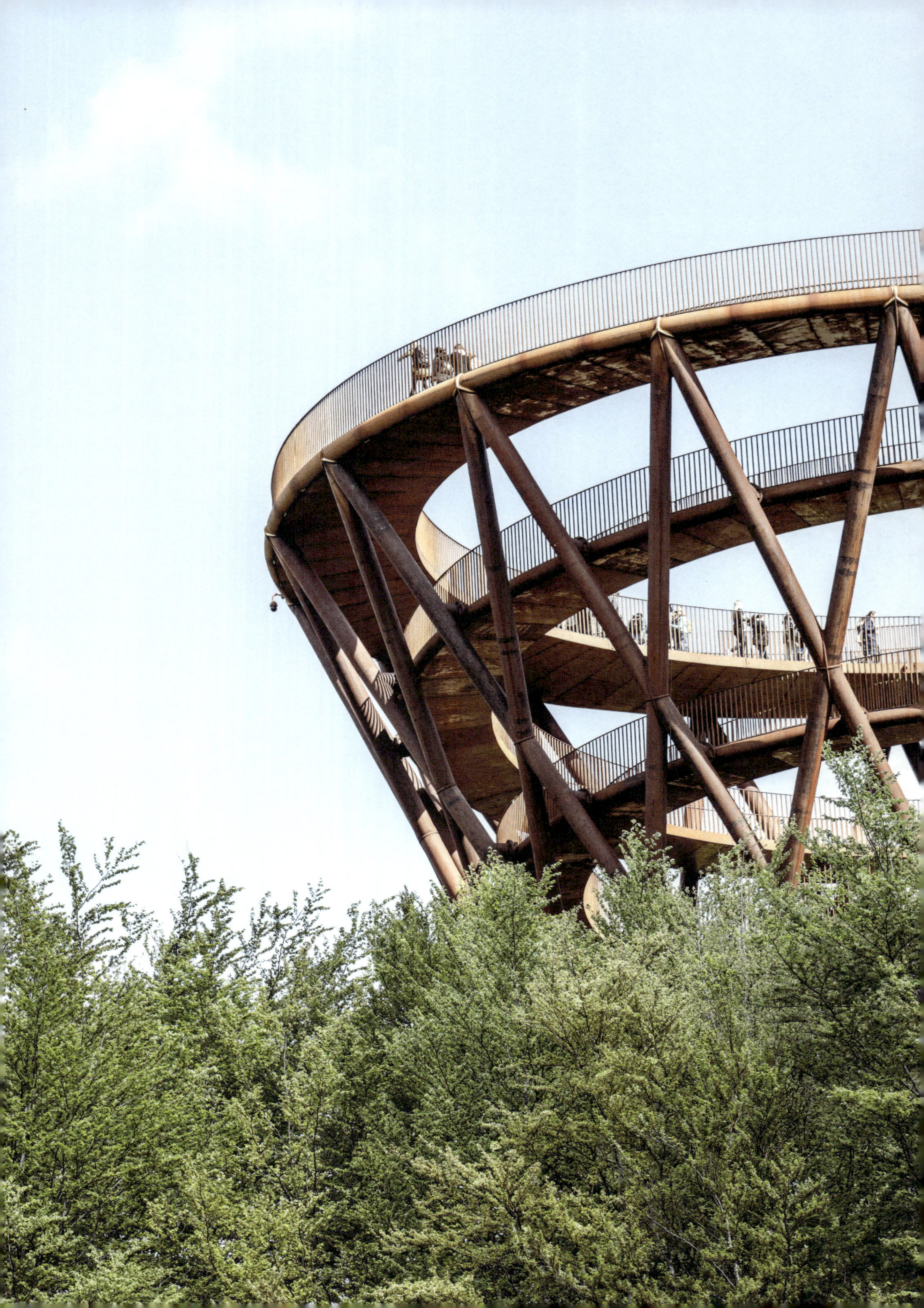

Architecture as Signature

Tue Foged, partner at the architecture firm EFFEKT, interviewed by Kristoffer Lindhardt Weiss, director of the Danish Architectural Press

KLW Your architecture office was commissioned to design an attraction to, essentially, highlight the forest experience. How did you approach the project?

TF We have so little woodland in Denmark, and it is actually the type of natural setting that most Danes prefer to visit when they want to experience nature. Denmark has one of the longest coastlines of any country in Europe – 8,700 kilometres. Nevertheless, only about 40 million people a year visit the coast, while 70 million visit a wood. That says a lot about the type of nature we generally wish to experience. So the natural question was, how can we give Danes access to the forest experience without adding pressure to its ecosystems? That was our focus throughout the design process. We were excited to see that when Danish TV staged the world's first national televised fundraiser to fight climate change in autumn 2019, the Forest Tower was selected as the setting. In just a few months, it had become a symbol of the forest as a valuable attraction and a key part of the solution in our global climate discussion. That is why we find it so crucial to make people appreciate and protect nature.

KLW Building in a forest might seem quite intrusive but could in fact be just the opposite?

TF The client, Camp Adventure, wanted to give more people access to a new kind of forest experience. And the Danish Nature Agency saw the point of the tower as a different way to convey the qualities and experiences the woods have to offer. So the brief was to create a design that attracts many people and provides full access for all user groups – and to do it in way that does no harm to the wood. And also in a way that was surprising and which would stage the forest in a new way, adding a new experience. The project consists of a 3.2-kilometre-long forest path with the tower in the middle of the route as a vertical experience that takes people from the forest floor up through the tree crowns and further up, above the trees, where they can look out over the forest. It is a new way of seeing the forest. On a clear day, in addition to overlooking the landscape of southern Zealand, you can see all the way to Copenhagen and Malmö. You can almost see the curvature of the earth. Offering an entirely new nature experience, unprecedented in Denmark, it has the potential to attract a lot of people.

KLW How would you describe the Forest Tower? What were your key design considerations?

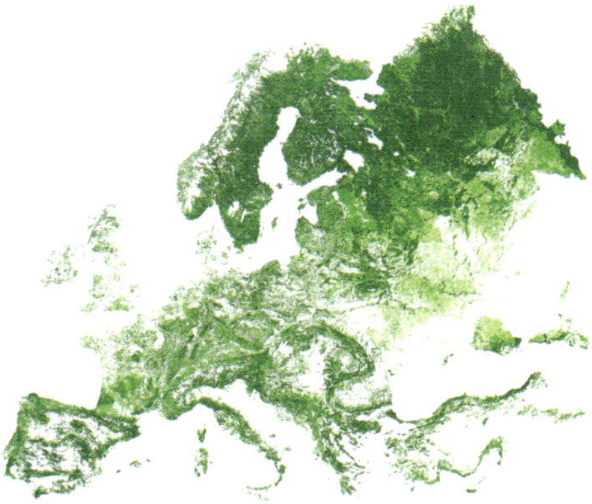

VS

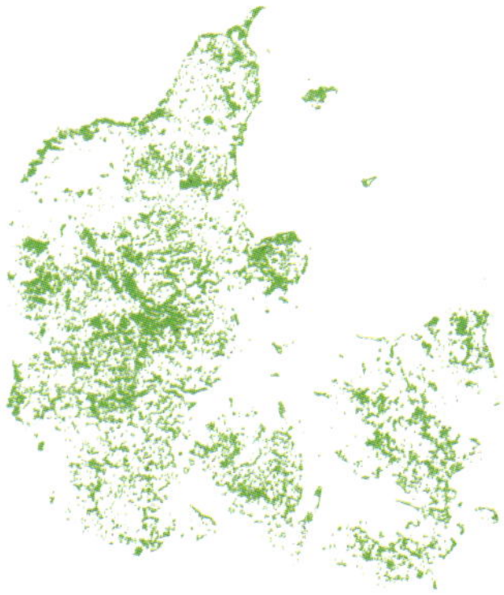

EU forest
45%
woodland

DK forest
11%
woodland

Denmark has only 0.09% of the EU's forest areas.

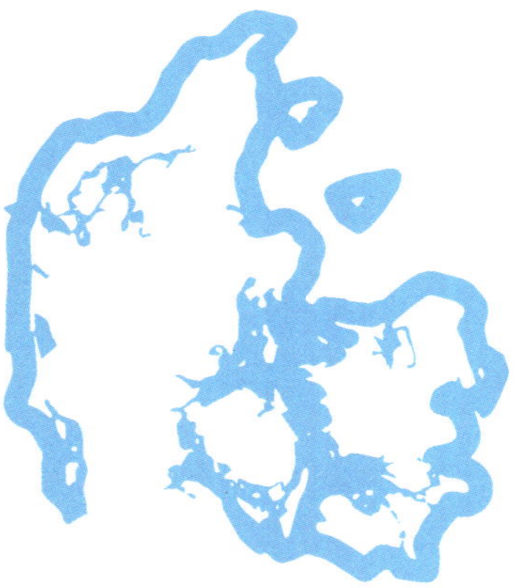

VS

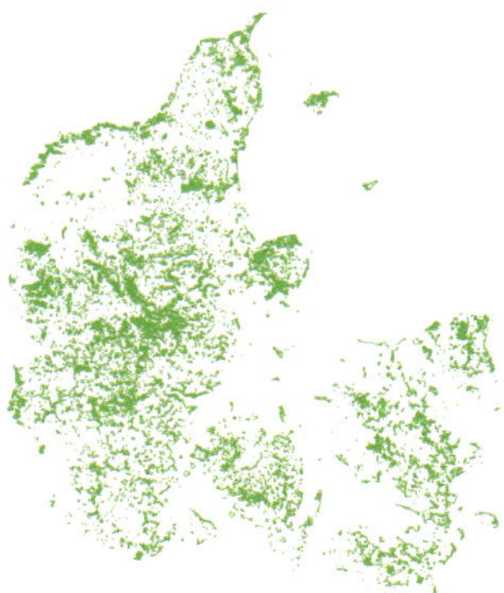

DK coast
40 million
visitors/year

DK forest
70 million
visitors/year

Although the country has a rich and varied coastline, woodlands are still the most visited natural destination.

TF The most important design consideration was to offer a novel experience and also a continuous experience that begins long before you arrive at the Forest Tower. So we approached the design from the point of view of building a tension curve for the overall experience in a dramaturgical, filmic approach. The arc begins long before you reach Camp Adventure, while you're still on the highway you see the Forest Tower rise above the forest in the distance. At this point, your expectations begin to build, as the sight offers an indication of the spectacular view you are about to enjoy. The experience builds further as you move down the footpath, weaving in among the trees in the forest. The point of no return is reached when you are at the foot of the Forest Tower itself, and the climax occurs on the top viewing platform where you are buffeted by the wind and have a 360-degree view of the forest. The experience then gradually tapers out as the return trip takes you back to your arrival point on a different route through the forest.

We also sought to address each of the many experiences and frequencies on its own terms in order to optimize every aspect of the overall experience. For example, we considered where people would be spending most time. In the Forest Tower itself, that is undoubtedly on the top platform, so it was important for us to make this a good experience for everyone, whether there were two visitors or a hundred visitors at the top. In the Eiffel Tower, the top platform is the smallest part of the entire construction – we did the exact opposite. In the Forest Tower, the top deck is the largest space. However, that placed high demands on the statics of the construction. We created a double-curvature construction that is incredibly stable and light; it's one of the most optimal constructions for supporting the top platform.

In addition to the arc of the experience, it was important for us to create a construction that is perceived as matching the natural setting, both in form and materiality. In a fine gesture towards the forest, the construction bends at the waist, bowing to the tree crowns and the forest around it. And inside, in the middle of the construction, we had room to preserve three trees. In that way, the forest is part of the experience both inside and outside the Forest Tower construction.

KLW Why does the construction look the way it does? It looks simultaneously highly complex and very simple.

TF The tower is 45 metres tall and consists of an exterior construction with a spiral ramp inside. The spiral is about 650 metres long – so the walk up and down again is almost a kilometre and a half. We wanted a ramp to make sure everyone had access to the same experience of moving inside the tower – including people with prams and wheelchairs. The ramp is a continuation of the footpath that leads to the tower, so in fact, you simply continue on the same route, only now going up. That establishes a seamless connection between the horizontal forest path and the vertical forest path. It's an amazing experience to glide up the ramp rather than climbing a stair or taking a lift. That would ruin the whole idea. The mathematical term for the shape of the Forest Tower is a hyperbolic paraboloid. What's fascinating about it is that if you simply had a cylinder and

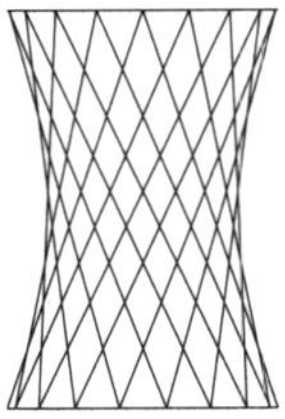

Rotation 90°
Top Ø 30 m
Central Ø 21 m
Base Ø 30 m
Height 45 m
Structure length 49.5 m
36 elements
Total structure length 1,790 m

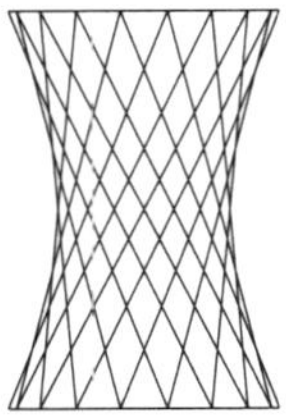

Rotation 100°
Top Ø 30 m
Central Ø 19.5 m
Base Ø 30 m
Height 45 m
Structure length 50.5 m
36 elements
Total structure length 1,819 m

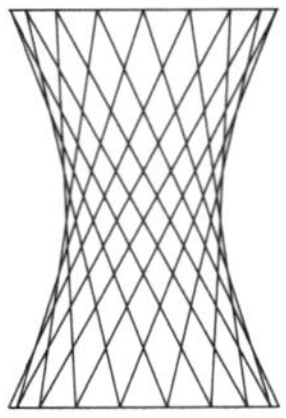

Rotation 110°
Top Ø 30 m
Central Ø 17.5 m
Base Ø 30 m
Height 45 m
Structure length 51 m
36 elements
Total structure length 1,846 m

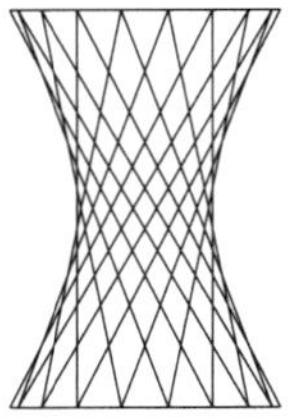

Rotation 120°
Top Ø 30 m
Central Ø 15 m
Base Ø 30 m
Height 45 m
Structure length 52 m
36 elements
Total structure length 1,875 m

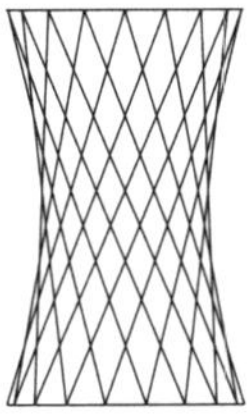

Rotation 90°
Top Ø 26.5 m
Central Ø 19 m
Base Ø 26.5 m
Height 45 m
Structure length 49 m
36 elements
Total structure length 1,752 m

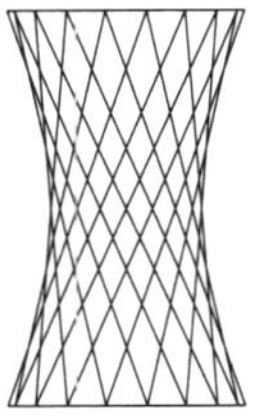

Rotation 100°
Top Ø 26.5 m
Central Ø 17 m
Base Ø 26.5 m
Height 45 m
Structure length 49.5 m
36 elements
Total structure length 1,774 m

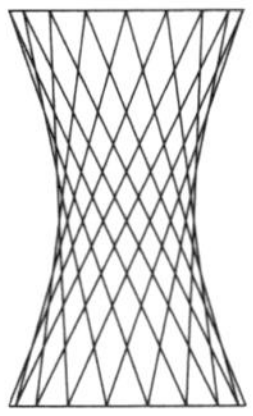

Rotation 110°
Top Ø 26.5 m
Central Ø 15 m
Base Ø 26.5 m
Height 45 m
Structure length 49.5 m
36 elements
Total structure length 1,796 m

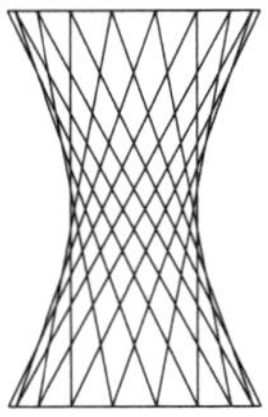

Rotation 120°
Top Ø 28 m
Central Ø 14 m
Base Ø 28 m
Height 45 m
Structure length 50.5 m
36 elements
Total structure length 1,815 m

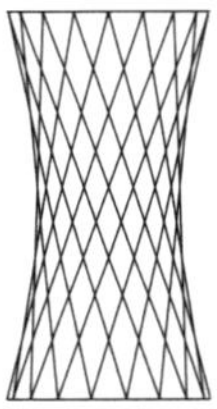

Rotation 90°
Top Ø 22.5 m
Central Ø 16 m
Base Ø 22.5 m
Height 45 m
Structure length 47.5 m
36 elements
Total structure length 1,718 m

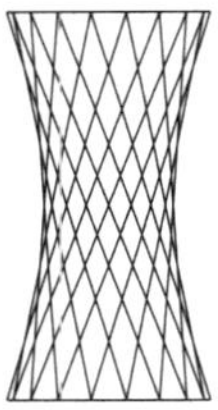

Rotation 100°
Top Ø 22.5 m
Central Ø 14.5 m
Base Ø 22.5 m
Height 45 m
Structure length 48 m
36 elements
Total structure length 1,735 m

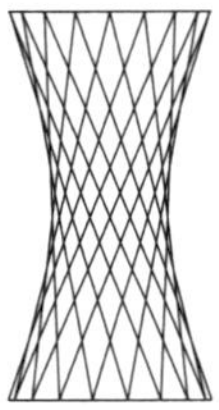

Rotation 110°
Top Ø 22.5 m
Central Ø 13 m
Base Ø 22.5 m
Height 45 m
Structure length 49 m
36 elements
Total structure length 1,751 m

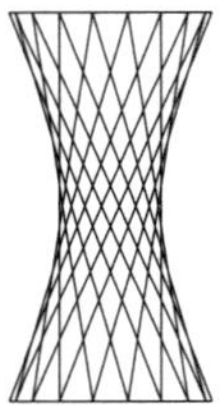

Rotation 120°
Top Ø 22.5 m
Central Ø 11.5 m
Base Ø 22.5 m
Height 45 m
Structure length 49 m
36 elements
Total structure length 1,763 m

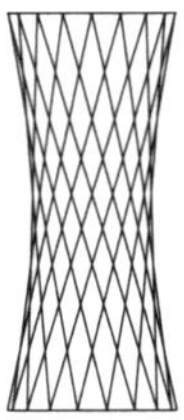

Rotation 90°
Top Ø 19 m
Central Ø 13.5 m
Base Ø 19 m
Height 45 m
Structure length 46.5 m
36 elements
Total structure length 1,688 m

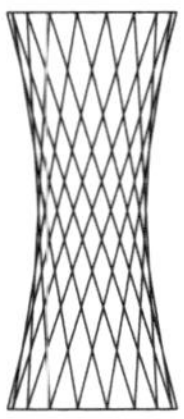

Rotation 100°
Top Ø 19 m
Central Ø 12 m
Base Ø 19 m
Height 45 m
Structure length 47.5 m
36 elements
Total structure length 1,700 m

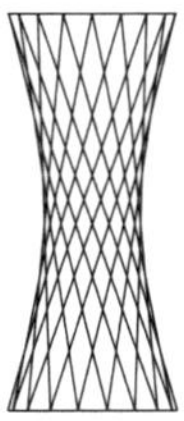

Rotation 110°
Top Ø 19 m
Central Ø 10.5 m
Base Ø 18.75 m
Height 45 m
Structure length 47.5 m
36 elements
Total structure length 1,712 m

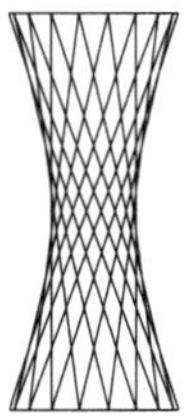

Rotation 120°
Top Ø 19 m
Central Ø 9.5 m
Base Ø 19 m
Height 45 m
Structure length 47.5 m
36 elements
Total structure length 1,722 m

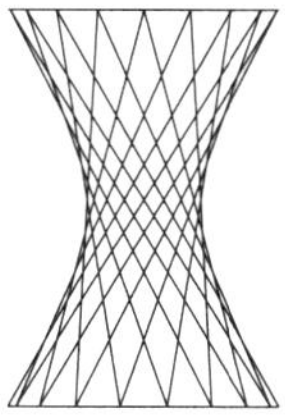

Rotation 130°
Top Ø 30 m
Central Ø 13 m
Base Ø 30 m
Height 45 m
Structure length 52.5 m
36 elements
Total structure length 1,892 m

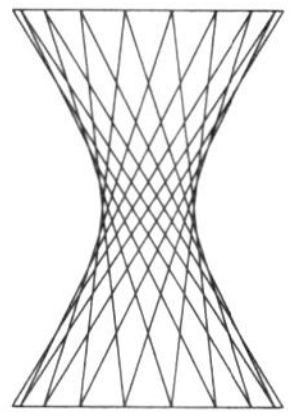

Rotation 140°
Top Ø 30 m
Central Ø 10.5 m
Base Ø 30 m
Height 45 m
Structure length 53.5 m
36 elements
Total structure length 1,911 m

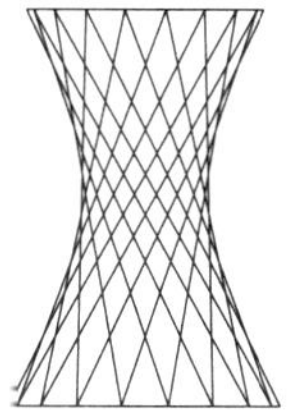

Rotation 120°
Top Ø 26.5 m
Central Ø 13.5 m
Base Ø 30 m
Height 45 m
Structure length 51 m
36 elements
Total structure length 1,842 m

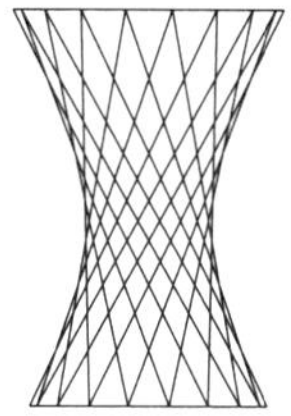

Rotation 120°
Top Ø 30 m
Central Ø 13.5 m
Base Ø 26.5 m
Height 45 m
Structure length 51 m
36 elements
Total structure length 1,842 m

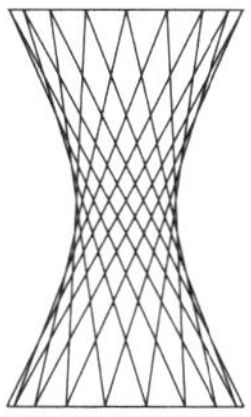

Rotation 130°
Top Ø 26.5 m
Central Ø 11.5 m
Base Ø 26.5 m
Height 45 m
Structure length 51 m
36 elements
Total structure length 1,832 m

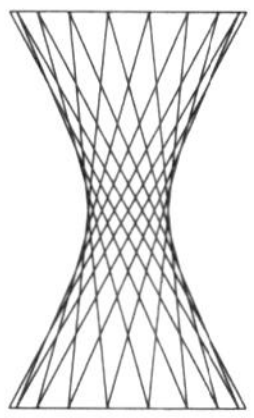

Rotation 140°
Top Ø 26.5 m
Central Ø 9 m
Base Ø 26.5 m
Height 45 m
Structure length 51 m
36 elements
Total structure length 1,847 m

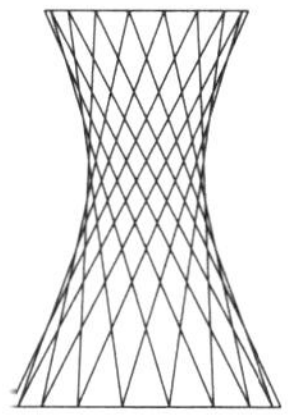

Rotation 120°
Top Ø 22.5 m
Central Ø 13 m
Base Ø 30 m
Height 45 m
Structure length 50.5 m
36 elements
Total structure length 1,816 m

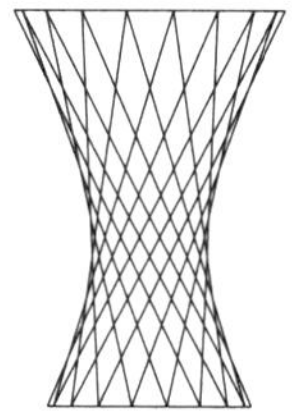

Rotation 120°
Top Ø 30 m
Central Ø 13 m
Base Ø 22.5 m
Height 45 m
Structure length 50.5 m
36 elements
Total structure length 1,816 m

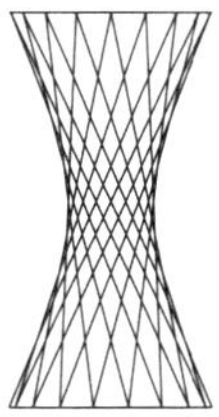

Rotation 130°
Top Ø 22.5 m
Central Ø 10 m
Base Ø 22.5 m
Height 45 m
Structure length 49.5 m
36 elements
Total structure length 1,778 m

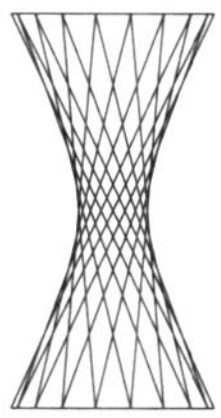

Rotation 140°
Top Ø 22.5 m
Central Ø 7.5 m
Base Ø 22.5 m
Height 45 m
Structure length 49.5 m
36 elements
Total structure length 1,789 m

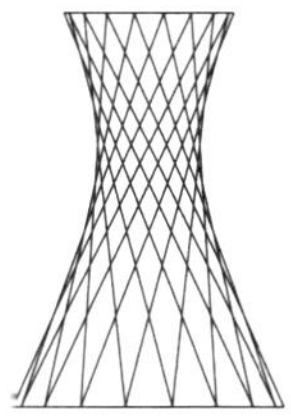

Rotation 120°
Top Ø 19 m
Central Ø 11.5 m
Base Ø 30 m
Height 45 m
Structure length 49.5 m
36 elements
Total structure length 1,792 m

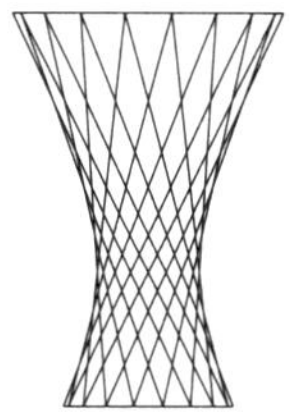

Rotation 120°
Top Ø 30 m
Central Ø 11.25 m
Base Ø 19 m
Height 45 m
Structure length 49.5 m
36 elements
Total structure length 1,792 m

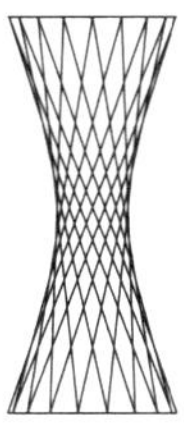

Rotation 130°
Top Ø 19 m
Central Ø 7.5 m
Base Ø 19 m
Height 45 m
Structure length 48 m
36 elements
Total structure length 1,731 m

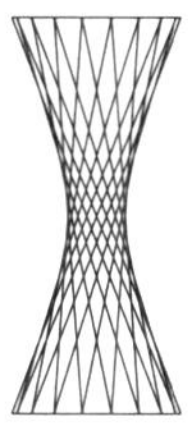

Rotation 140°
Top Ø 19 m
Central Ø 6.3 m
Base Ø 19 m
Height 45 m
Structure length 48 m
36 elements
Total structure length 1,739 m

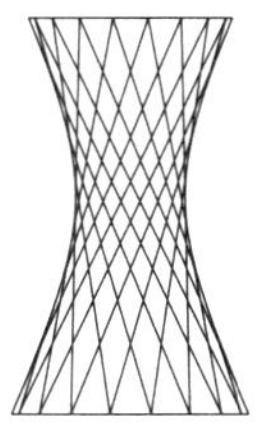

Rotation 120°
Top Ø 22.5 m
Central Ø 12 m
Base Ø 26.5 m
Height 45 m
Structure length 49.5 m
36 elements
Total structure length 1,790 m

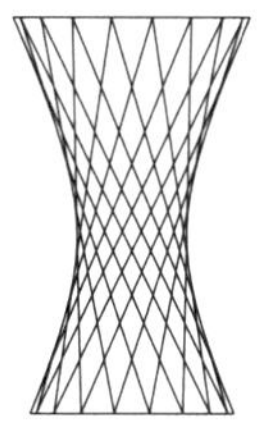

Rotation 120°
Top Ø 26.5 m
Central Ø 12 m
Base Ø 22.5 m
Height 45 m
Structure length 49.5 m
36 elements
Total structure length 1,790 m

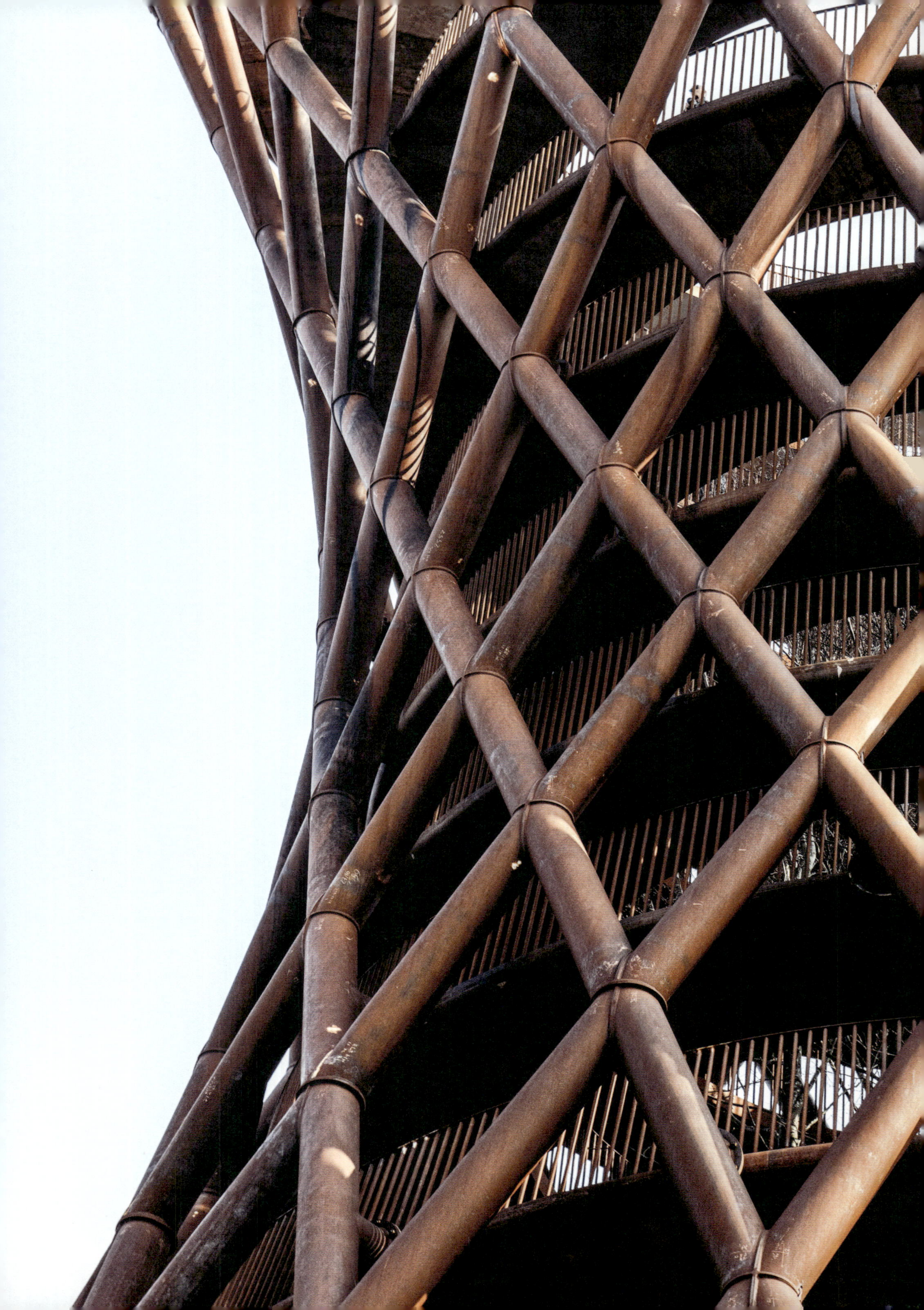

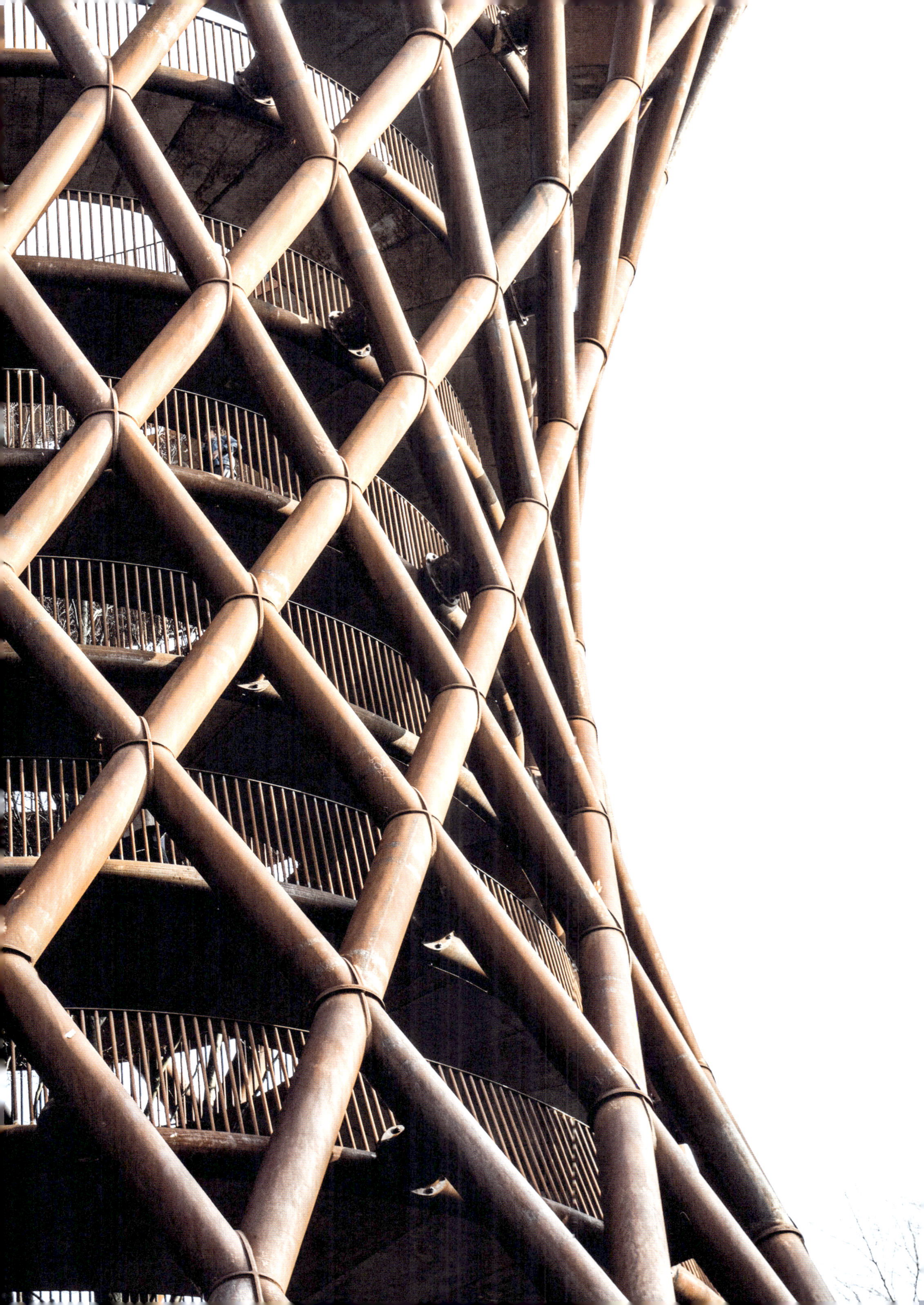

a ramp with 12 hoops you would be able to reach the same 360-degree platform at the top. But we deformed it, rotating the construction in order to stabilize it. We took 36 straight steel pipes and rotated every second pipe 120 degrees in one direction and the other pipes 120 degrees in the other direction, so that they cross. Then we stood them up and welded them into place, so they're completely straight.

We strapped a belt round the middle and pulled it in at the waist. To maintain a constant slope, we let the ramp deform in the middle of the construction. That offers a unique spatial sensation. Thus, when you enter the Forest Tower, the construction is very open, and the gap from the first tier to the next is quite wide. As you approach the middle of the tower, the distance to the overhead level gradually shrinks until, finally, you can almost touch it, because the construction has been tightened so much, but the slope of the ramp remains unchanged. At the same time, the construction gets increasingly dense, gradually obstructing your view. In this way, it almost mimics the structure of the trees, with the openness of the bare trunks at the bottom and then the density of the tree crowns, where everything is compact and darker. Towards the top, the Forest Tower stretches out again as the distance between the levels expands, the construction becomes increasingly open, and you gradually have more light and a stronger impact from the wind moving through the tree crowns. All this intensifies the experience of moving into the open and provides a powerful spatial experience. When you reach the top, it is completely open; you have the full view and can feel the wind coming at you unhindered. That offers a very significant contrast to the compact experience you had just moments ago. Standing on the top, you can only see the middle of the structure, you can't see the bottom. Similarly, as you climb the tower, you can't see the top. You never see the whole tower at once, which is a pretty amazing thing, because it means you have to explore it and sense it with your body.

KLW Could you comment on your choice of materials – it makes for a very characteristic expression, where the colour and materiality make the tower seem part of the natural setting.

TF The Eiffel Tower is made of ordinary steel, which has to be repainted every year to withstand rust. So over the years, huge amounts of paint and time have gone into the maintenance of the tower. Our goal, with regard to the materiality of the tower, was to create something that we could place in nature where it would mostly take care of itself, with very little maintenance. To that end, we used a steel alloy called corten steel, which contains minerals that cause it to weather in a way where the rust itself forms a protective outer layer. This obviates the need for protective paint, and once it has developed this layer, it can be left alone for a century, maintaining its quality and colour. The construction has a rusty dark-brown to orange colour that we think is really beautiful in the forest, because it matches the trees in autumn and strikes a stunning contrast to the green tree crowns in spring and summer. We used just two materials for the tower: corten steel for the construction and sustainable, certified oak for the ramp inside the tower.

Cylinder
The objective of the original project was to build a wheelchair-accessible observation deck at an elevation of 45 metres above the surrounding landscape. The obvious geometric shape to support a continuous ramp to such a deck is the cylinder.

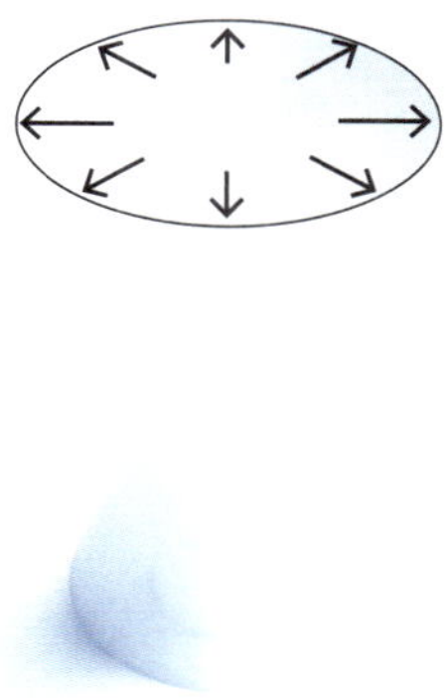

Maximizing footprint and top deck
The diameters of the base and top are maximized to increase the area of the observation deck to allow for more simultaneous visitors as well as as an increased footprint for improved stability.

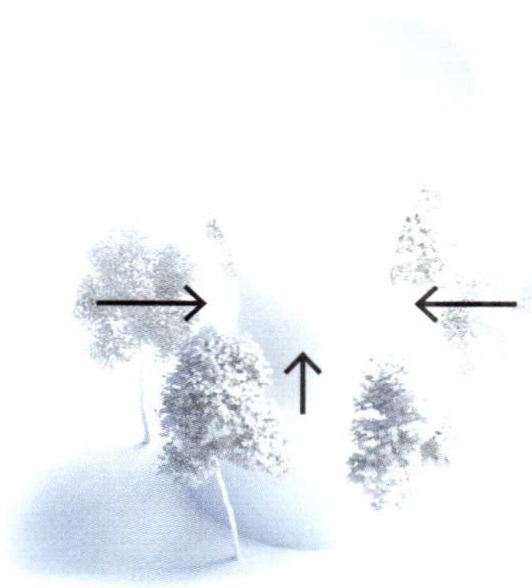

Improved contact
The hyperbolic curvature of the tower allows the crowns of the surrounding trees to grow closer to the spiralling path.

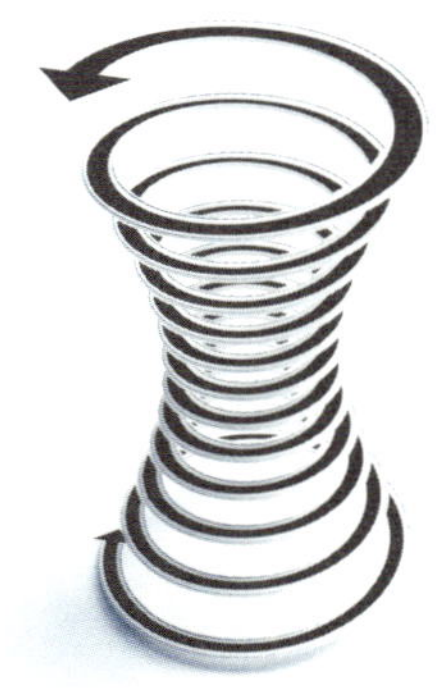

The ramp
A spiralling ramp with a continuous slope ensures accessibility to any visitor.

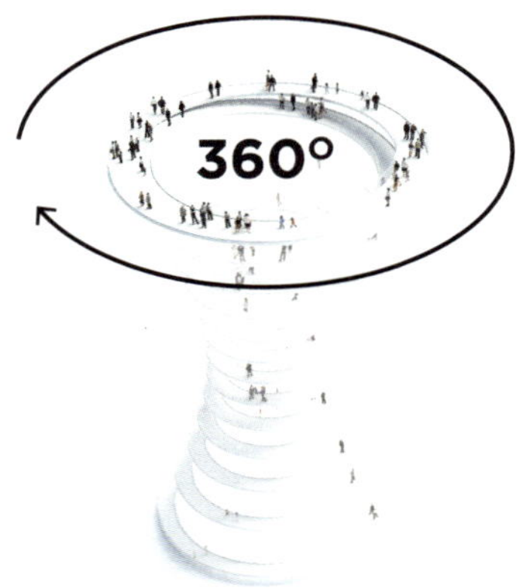

Observation deck
The observation deck offers a panoramic 360-degree view of the surrounding landscape and forest.

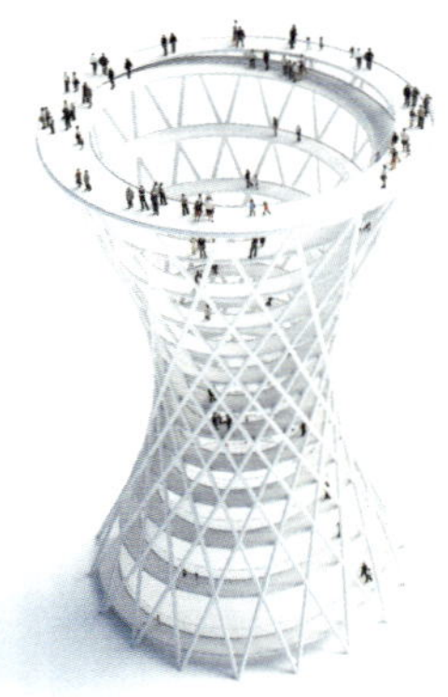

Experience
The tower enhances the experience of the visitors by providing a new perspective on nature in an enjoyable way.

KLW And you didn't cut down a single tree to create the footpath?

TF The forest path was built by Camp Adventure to follow the terrain and touch on certain select experiences as it crosses the river, runs along the brook and skirts the trees. Sometimes when it comes up against a tree, the edge of the path is adapted to the outline of the tree. In some cases, a hole was cut into the middle of the path to make room for a tree. So no trees were felled to create the path. On the ground, the path is made of pressure-treated, PEFC-certified pinewood, and the ramp that takes the visitors up into the tower is constructed of sustainable, PEFC-certified oak from the local estates Bregentved Gods and Gisselfeld Kloster.

KLW Why is this an important project to your architecture office?

TF It is important to us to have played a part in creating a place that people embrace from day one and which has the capacity to last for a very long time – and still be something that people appreciate. Many attractions are being Disneyfied these days – the Forest Tower is nothing like that. Our goal was to create a project that strikes a balance between the attraction and the location. An icon that stands up for itself but is still humble enough not to disturb its surroundings. You move through the forest, you ascend through the density of the tree crowns, and when you get to the top, what you experience is the sun and the wind. Throughout, the tower points to the elements and the setting. Denmark has a good minimalist design tradition. We sought to work in continuation of that tradition. Instead of creating an entirely new attraction – a Disneyfied experience – we sought to achieve a balance and a connection between the natural setting and the man-made features.

KLW I don't think I've seen it quite as clearly in other projects, this approach where the design is so distinct yet still allows room for the site that it's a part of.

TF The path leading to the tower is a key component. The build-up of expectations. It is a very straightforward way to provide a good experience. A walk in a wood seems to clear the mind. It's important that the tower is placed some distance away from the arrival area, so you have to make an effort to get to it.

KLW And what about the specific location of the tower?

TF There is actually a part of the forest that's even older. The tower is placed in the newer section, but it is the highest point in the area. It made sense to place the tower here, so we didn't have to add height to achieve the stunning views. Another reason why the tower is where it is, is that it was close to an existing service road. That may seem trivial, but it meant we didn't need to build new infrastructure during the construction phase, which further lessened the impact on the forest trees and ecosystems. Thus, the environmental concerns were a factor throughout, both in the finished design and in the planning of the construction process.

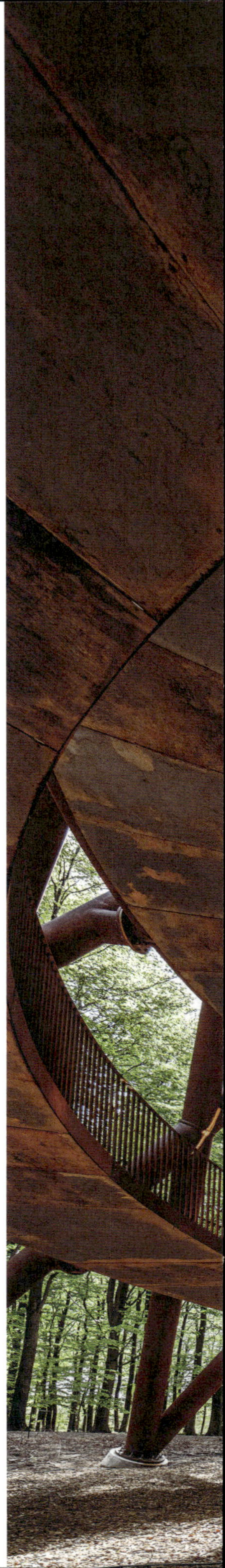

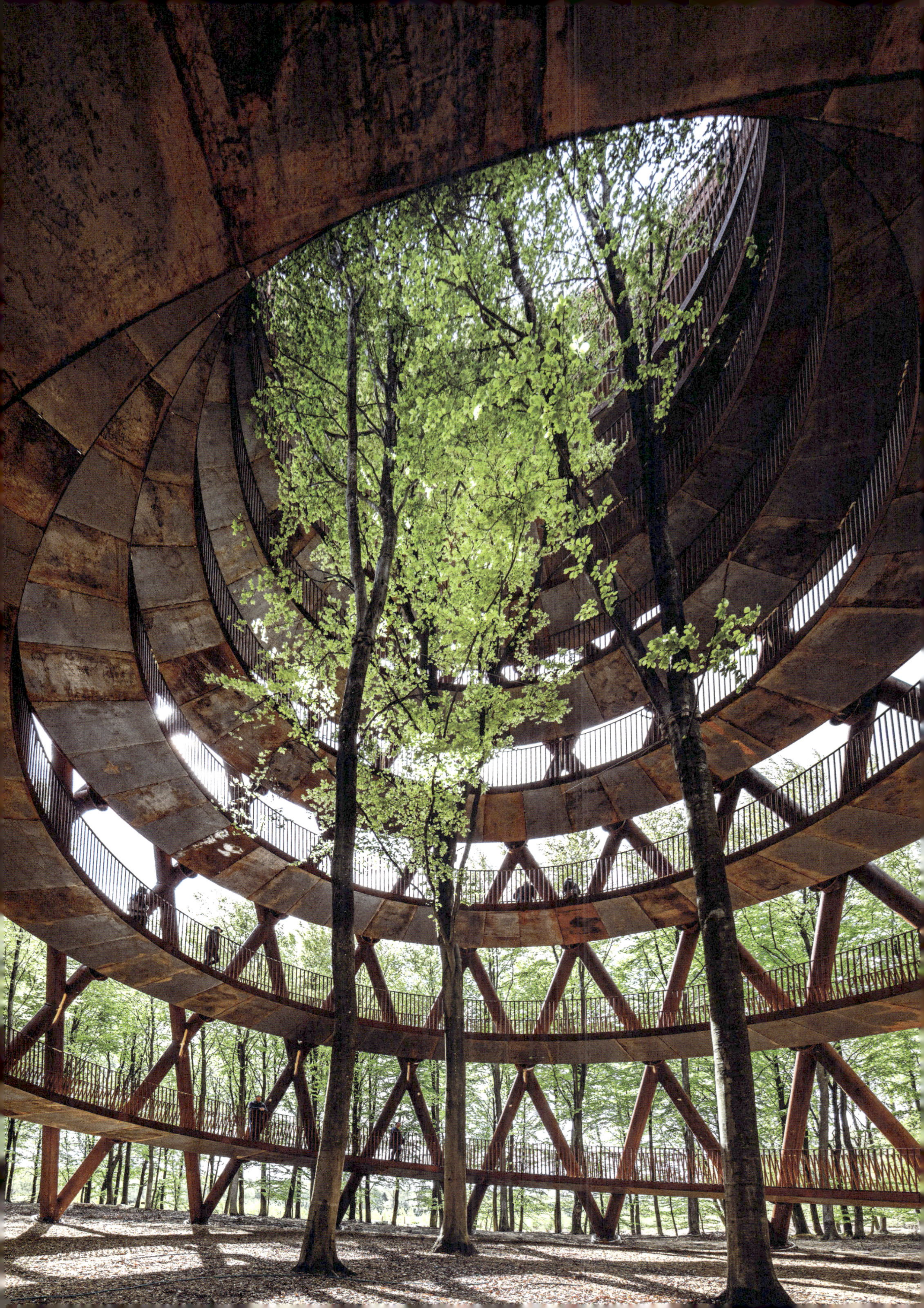

KLW You could not have designed the Forest Tower without the use of advanced software?

TF Today, it's possible to computer-generate countless different solutions. We used parametric design, where, instead of 3D-modelling 100 different variants of a form, we program the form algorithmically. You describe the form in mathematical terms. First, you design the form, and then you describe it mathematically. Nature is fascinating, and there is mathematics everywhere – in a pine cone, in a conch shell ... There is an almost mythical connection between nature's proportions and the way things deform in a conch shell, a pine cone and so forth, that is fascinating to the human mind. We perceive it as beauty. However, the parametric model soon became incredibly complex. The intention of maintaining the same ramp slope all the way from the forest floor to the viewing platform at the top while also adhering to the construction of the diagrid was difficult to describe in mathematical terms. The project architect posted the question in an online user forum on the program website to enlist the help of users around the world. First, David Rutten – the creator and lead developer of the parametric modelling tool Grasshopper at Robert McNeel & Associates – tried to find a solution. He almost managed, but ultimately, Ethan W. Gross, a 3D artist from Brooklyn, was the one who cracked the code of the complex model.

We were able to use the resulting parametric model to manage design and budget adjustments going forward and as the basis of the engineering firm Arup's static calculations. The complexity of the model was further confirmed when we were contacted, two months prior to the opening, by two professors at Politecnico di Milano, who had used our model to study the link between complex geometries and architecture.

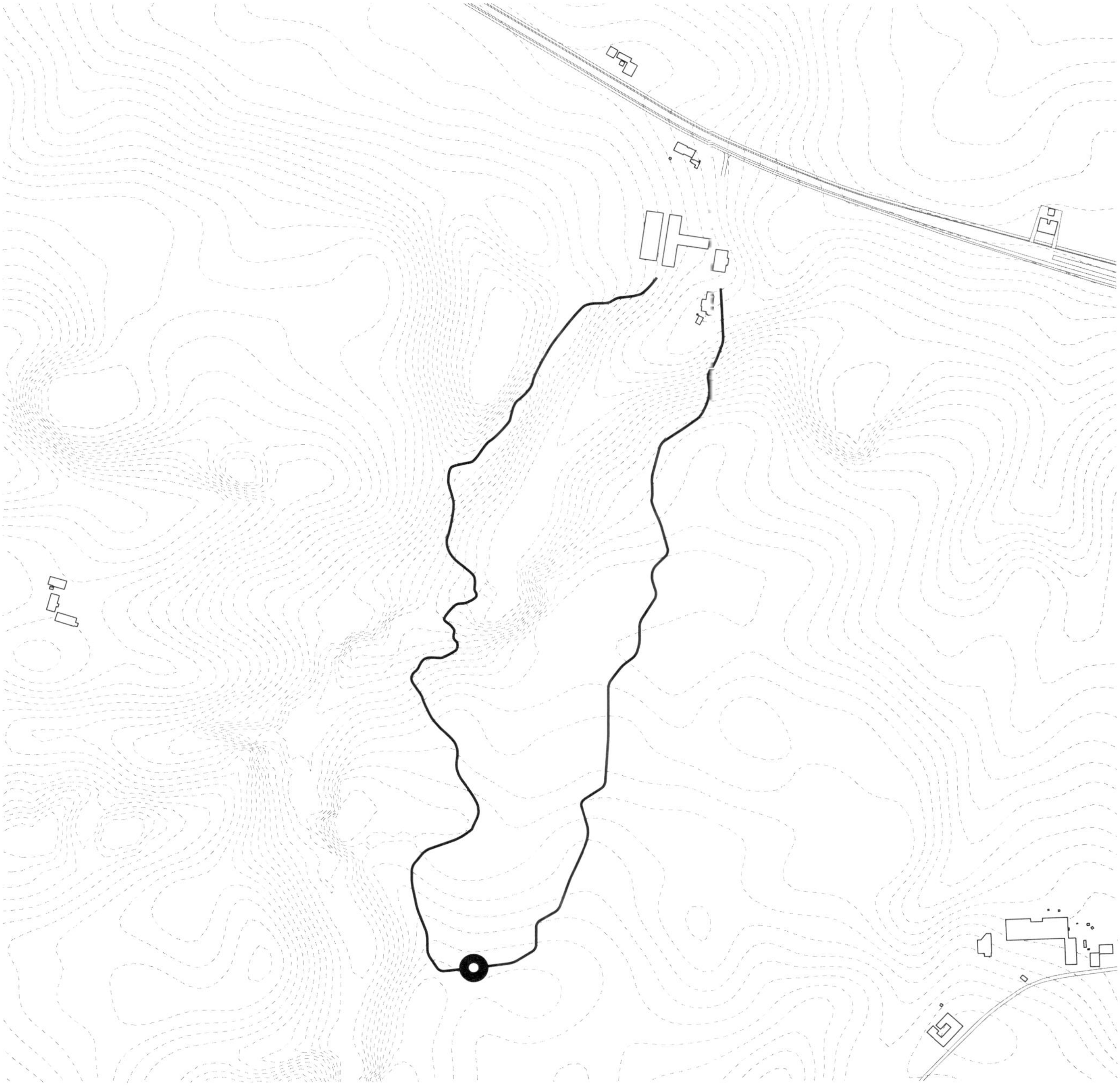

From the arrival area, visitors move through the protected forest to reach the Forest Tower, which occupies a strategic location in the landscape.

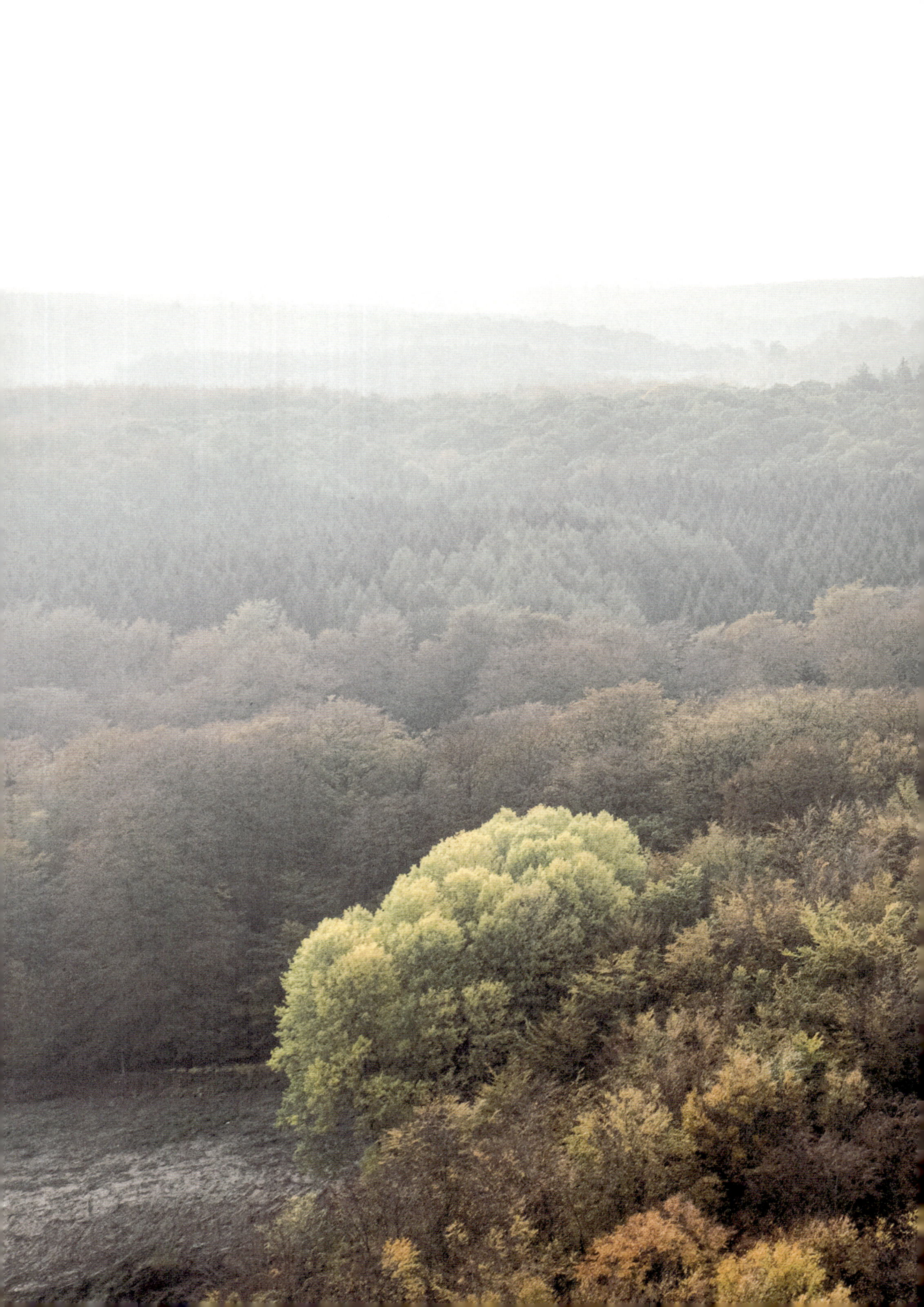

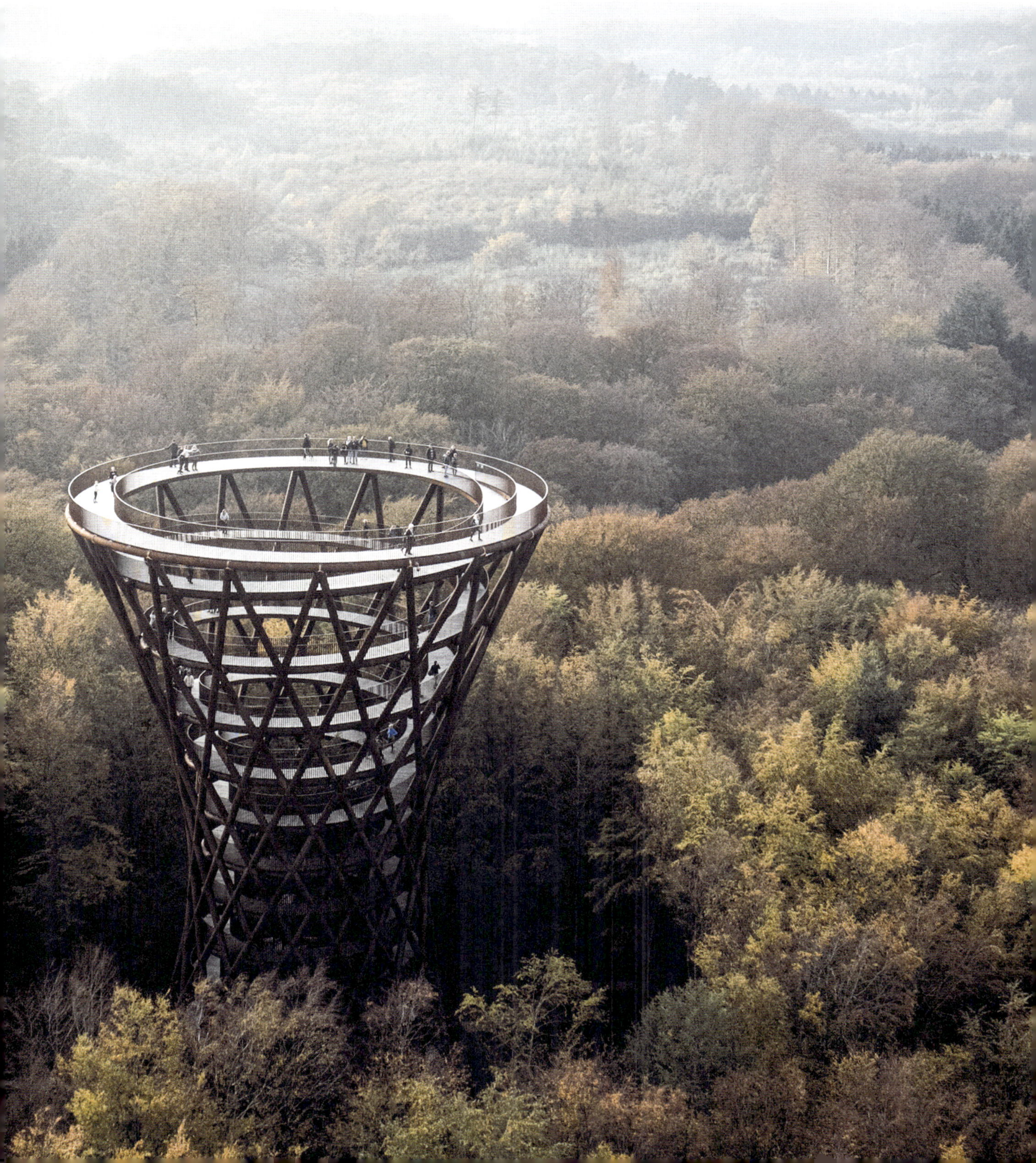

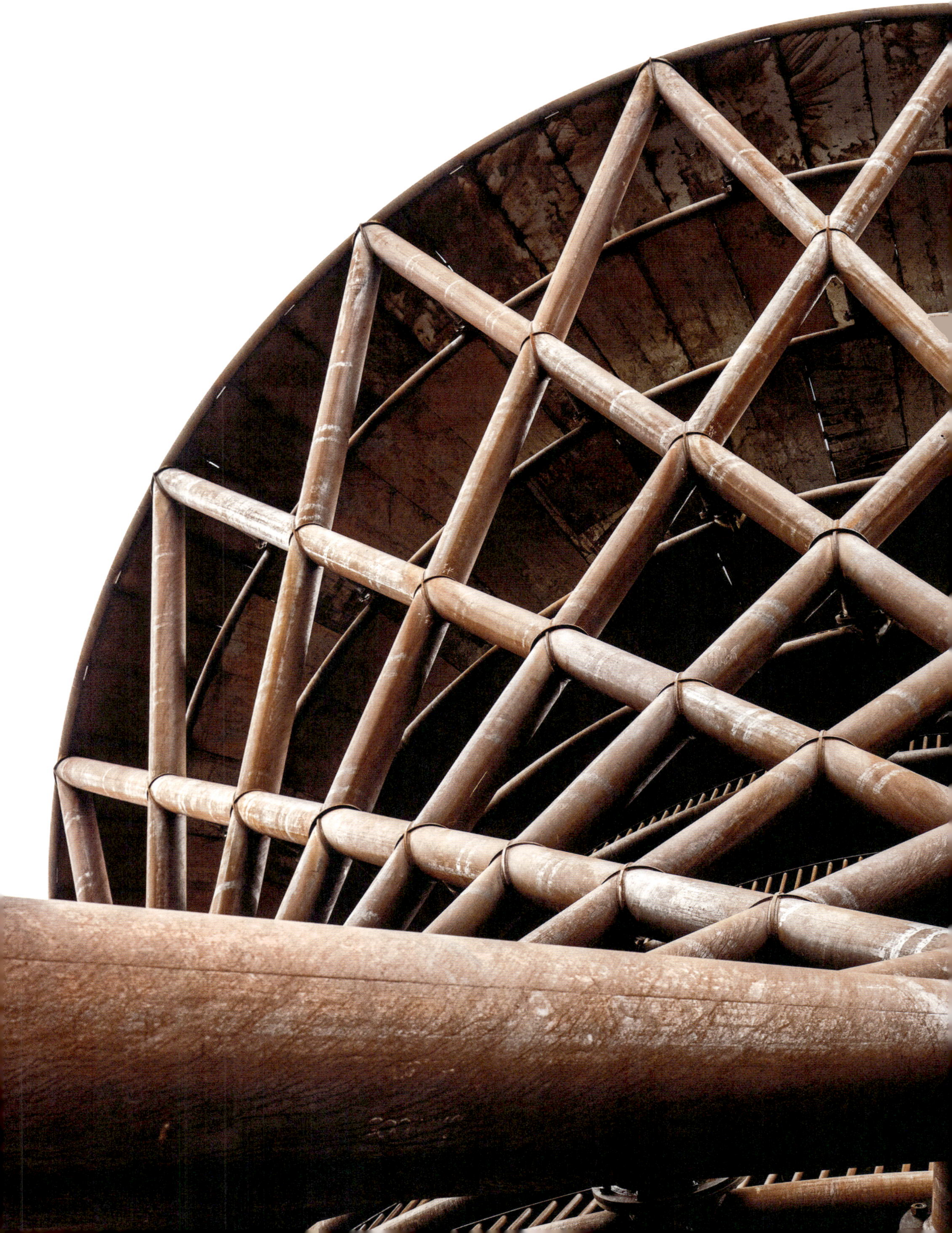

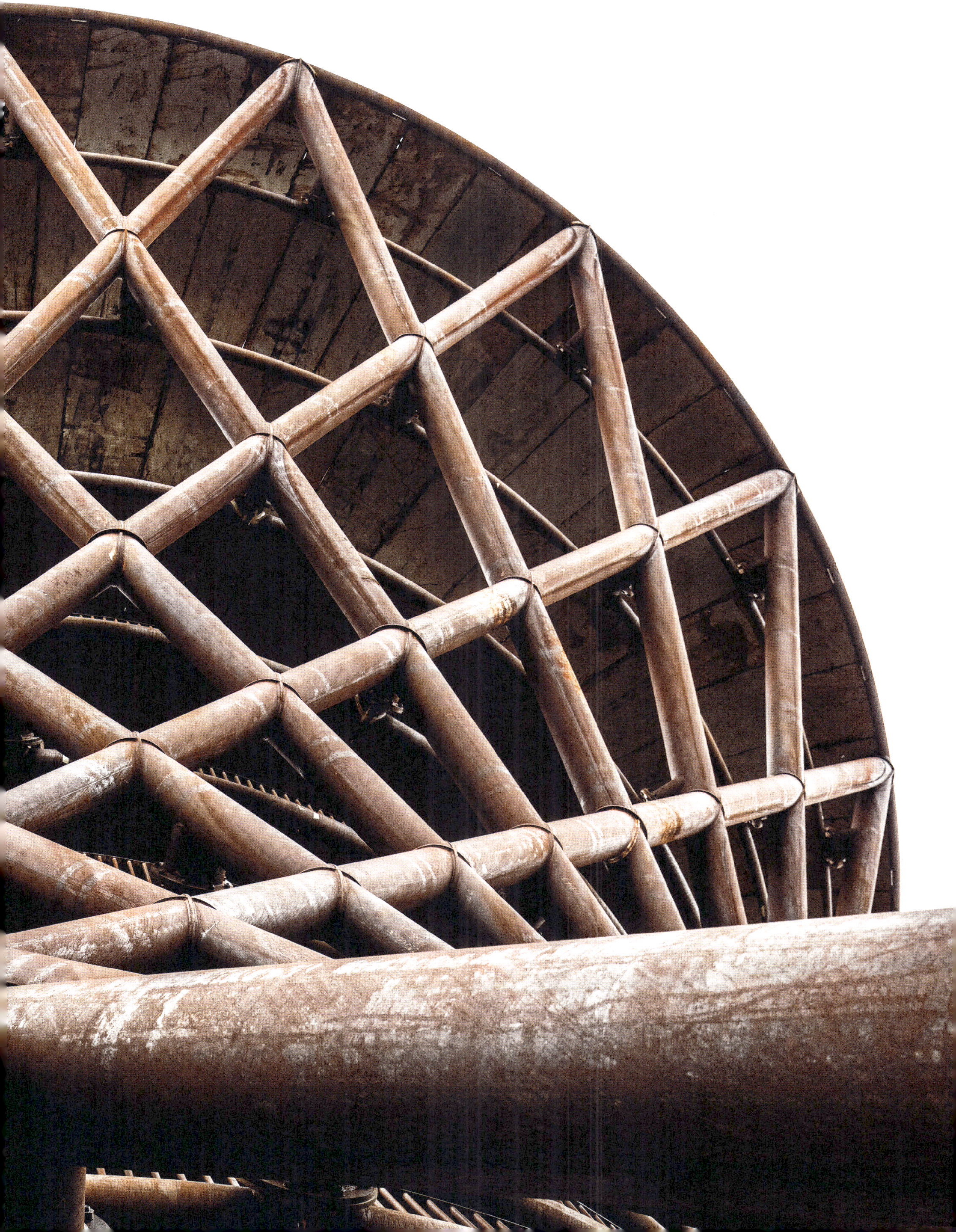

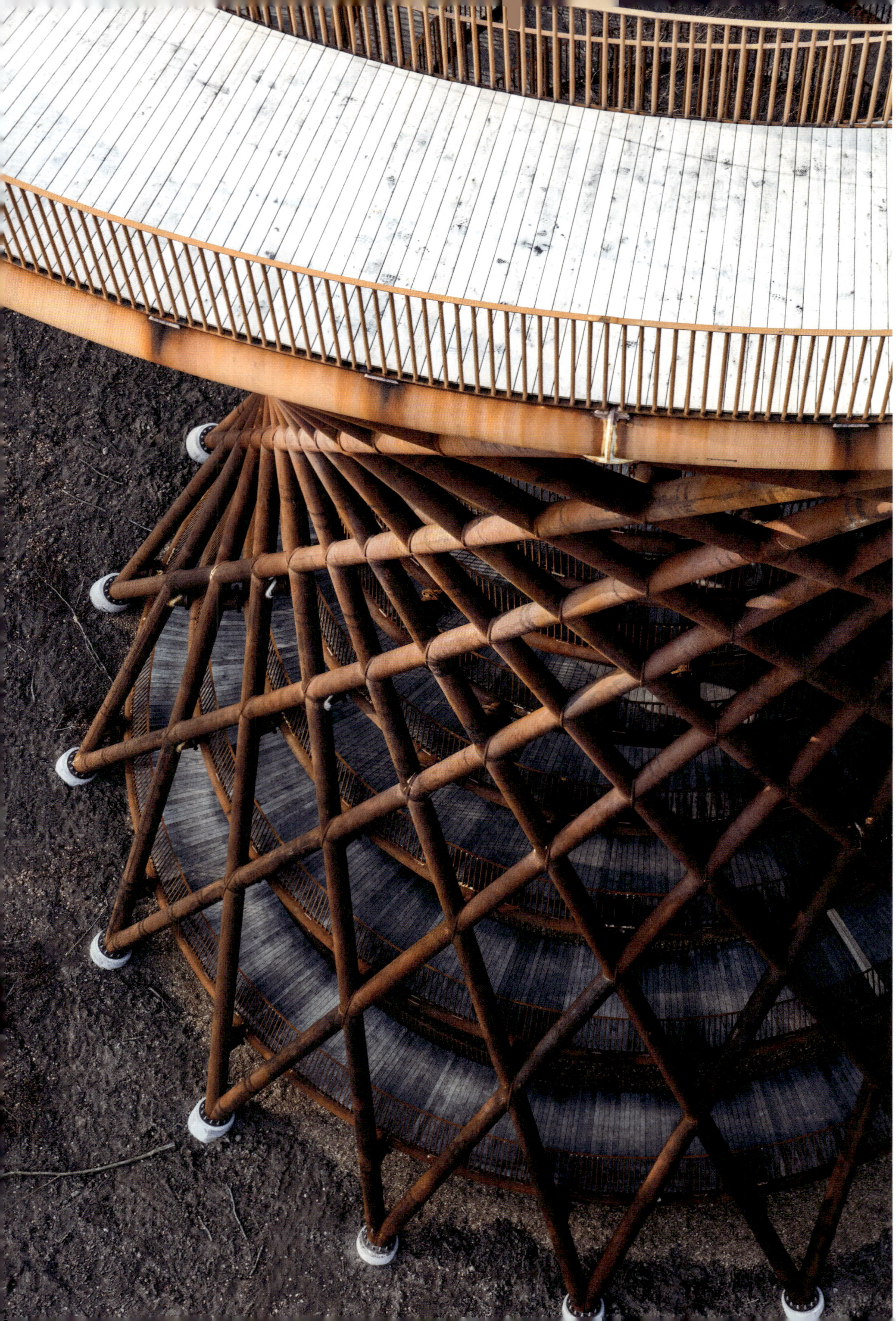

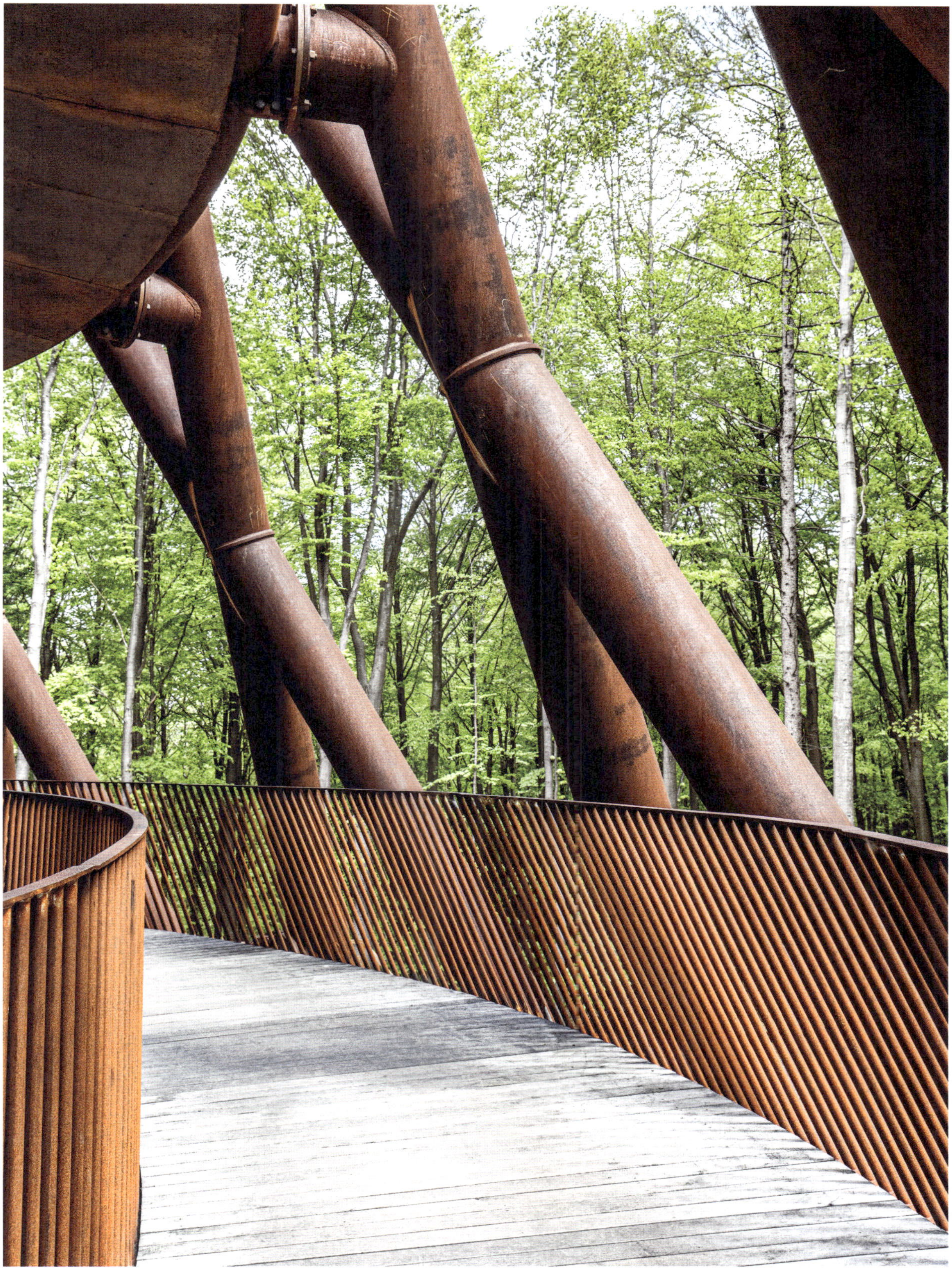

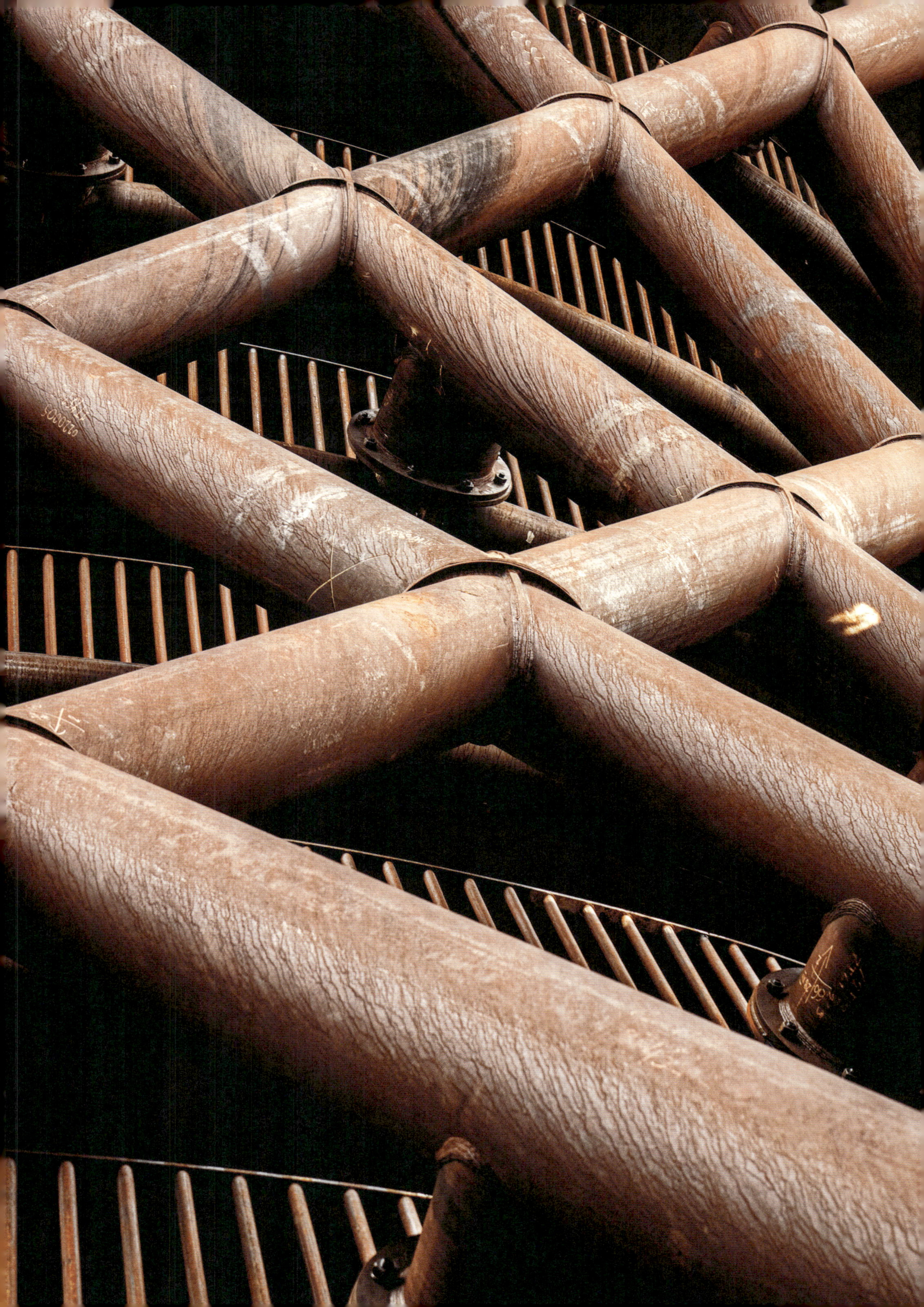

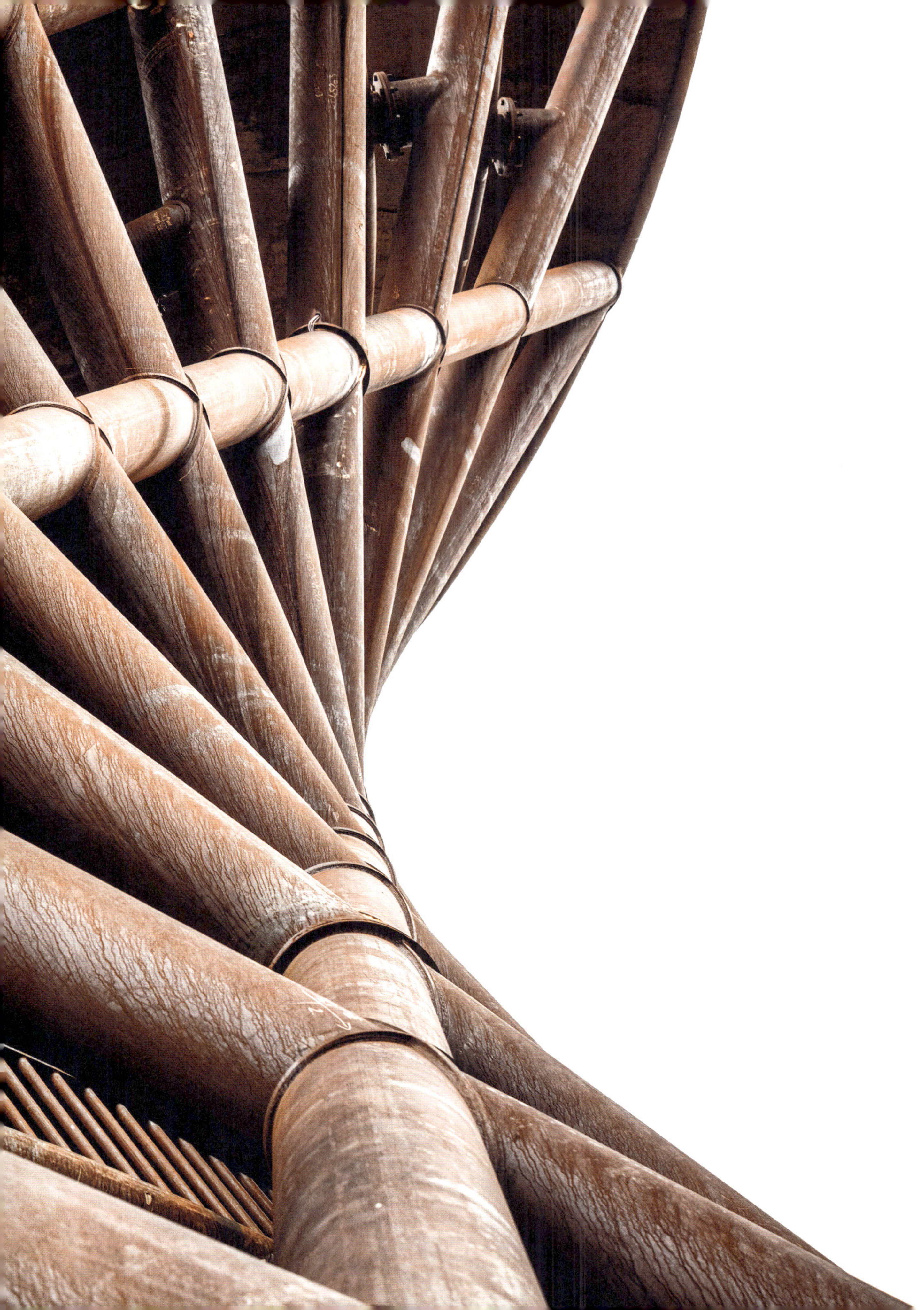

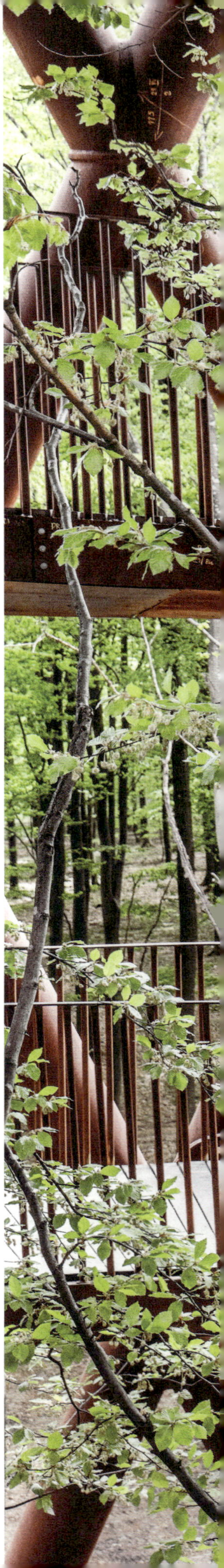

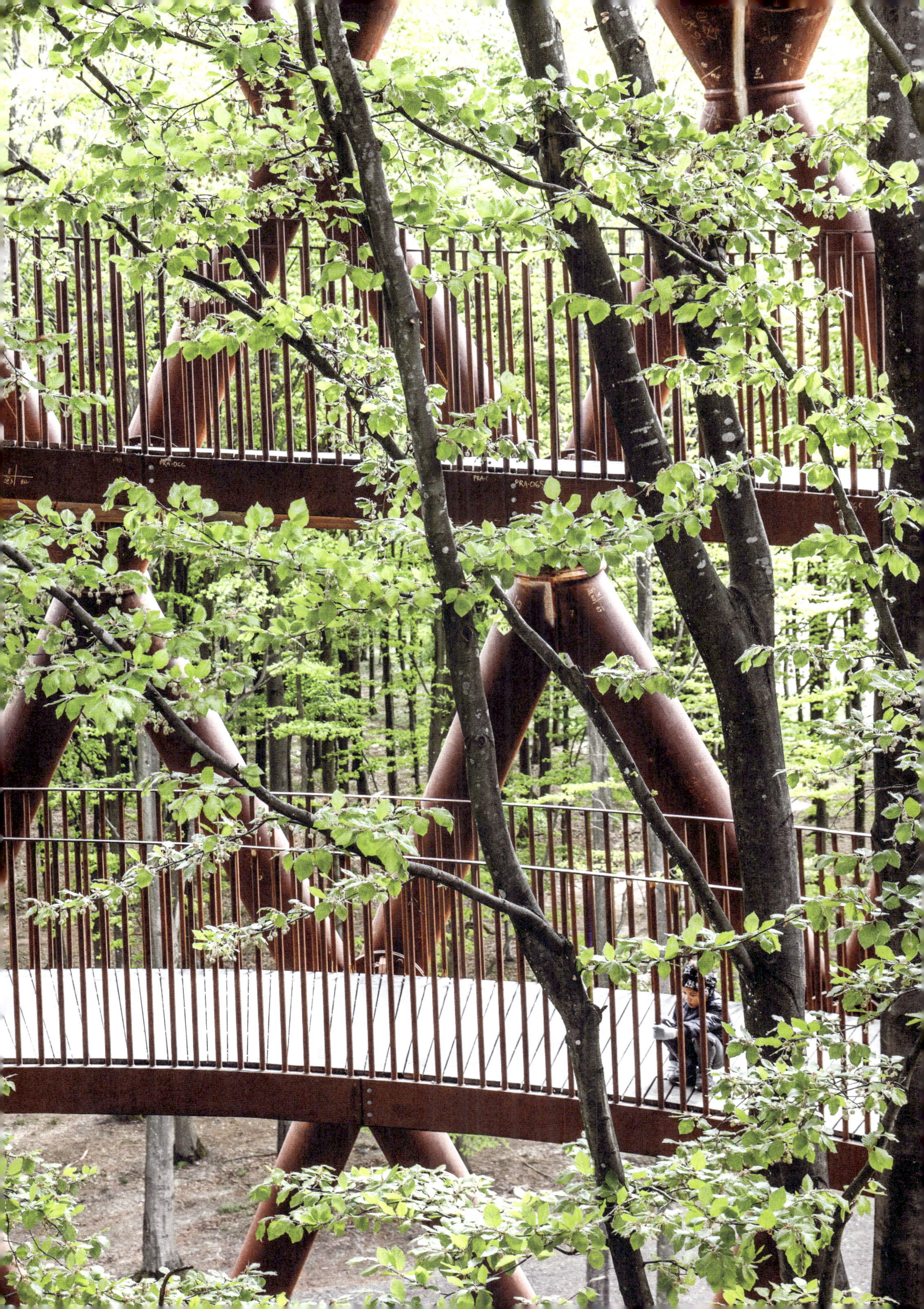

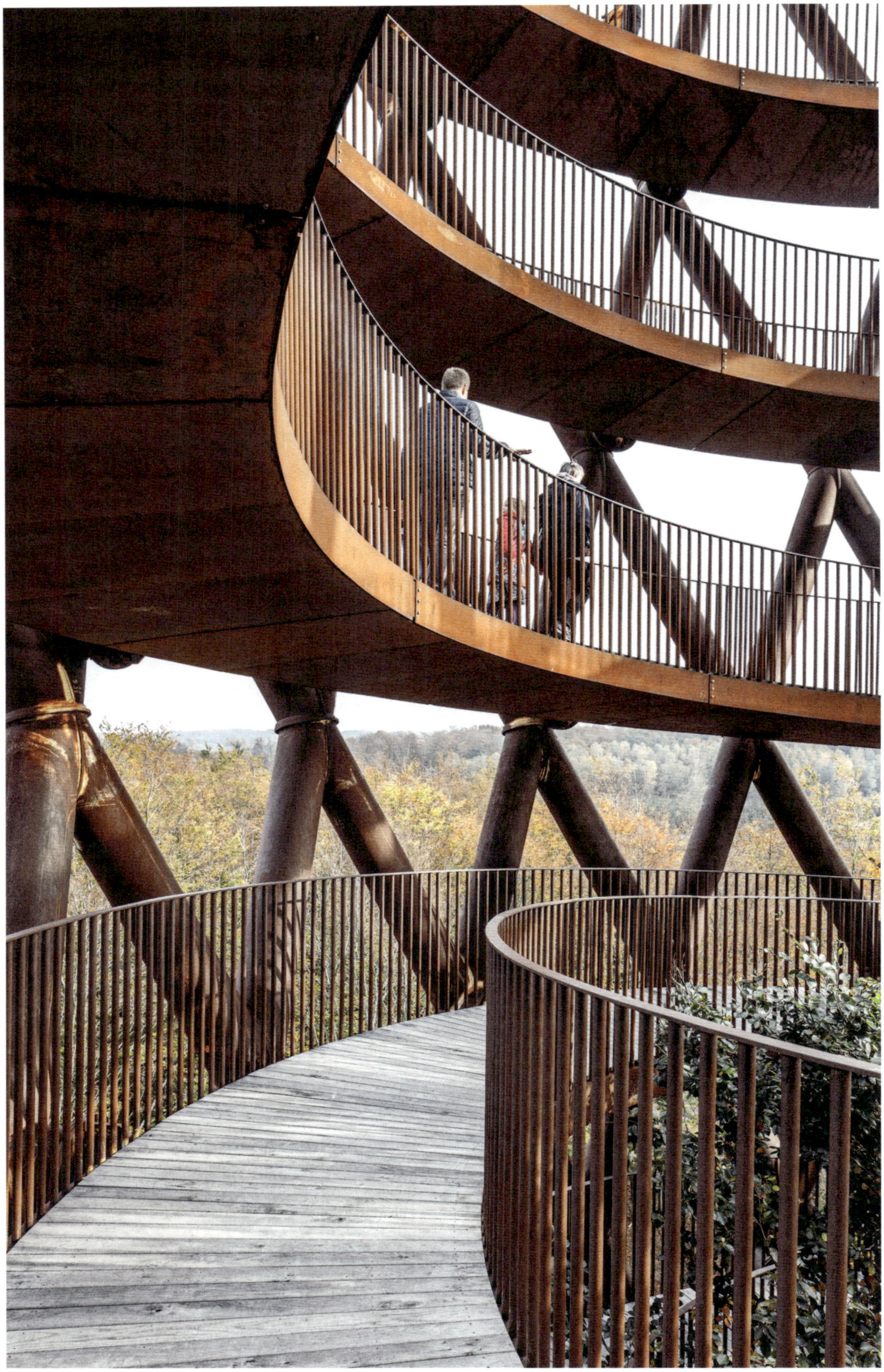

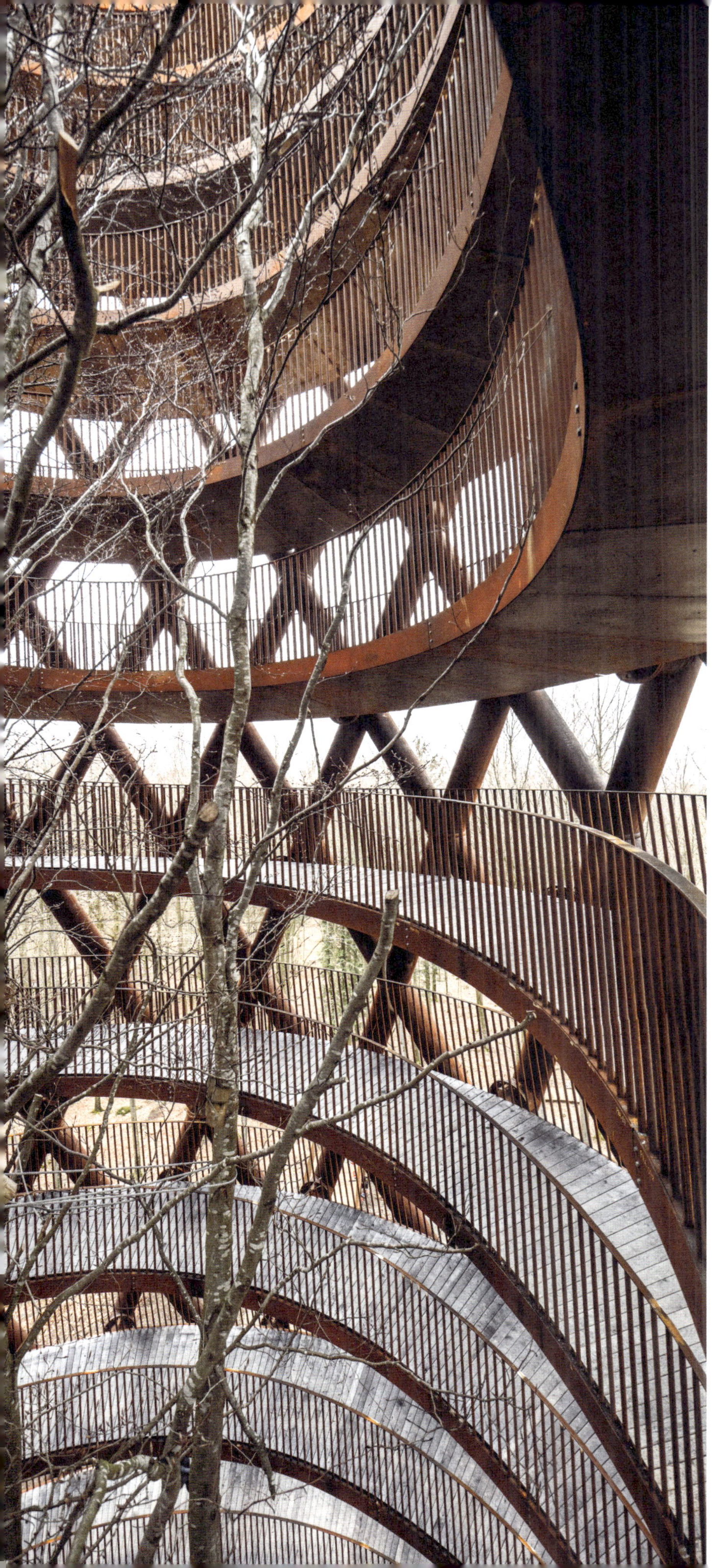

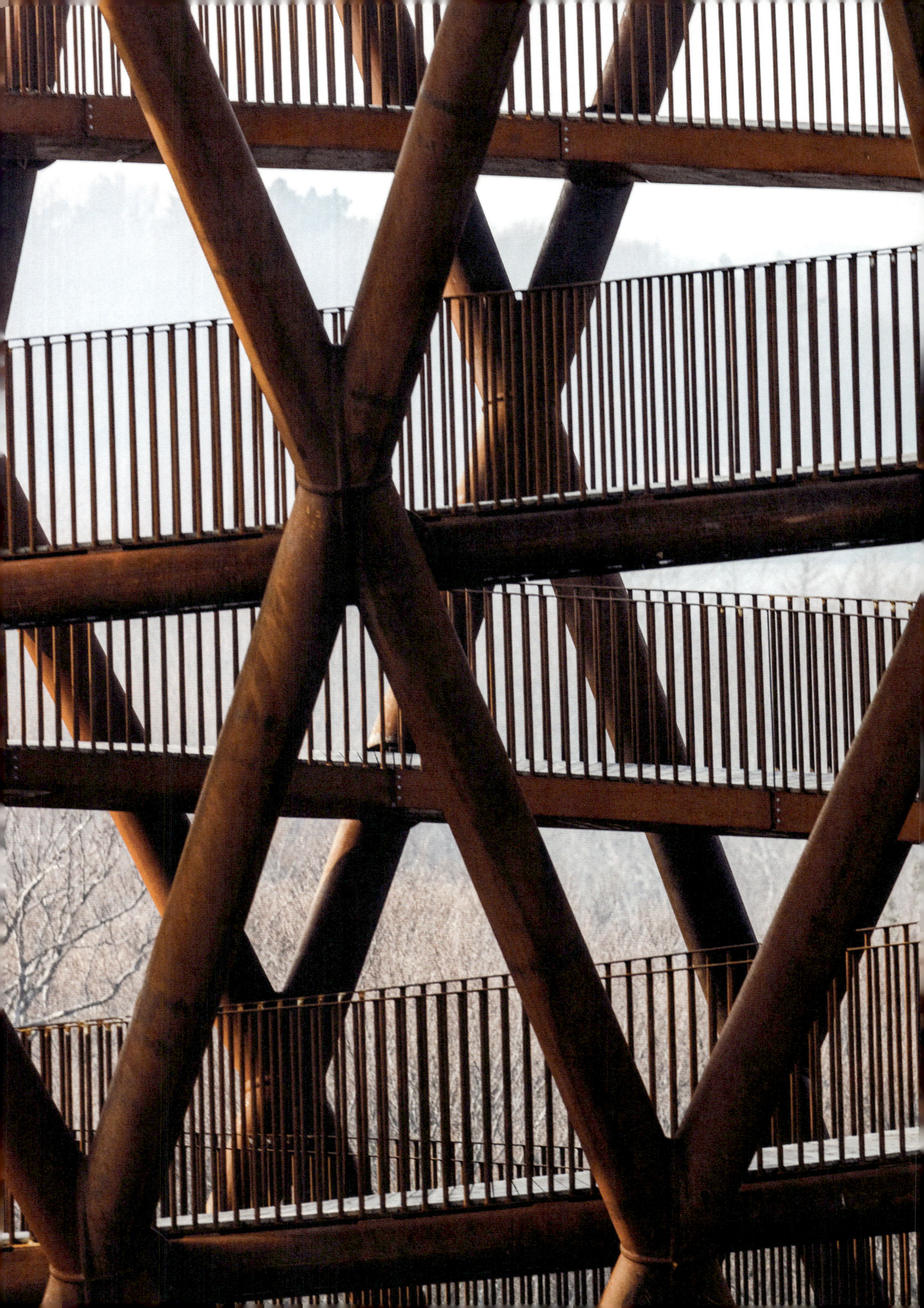

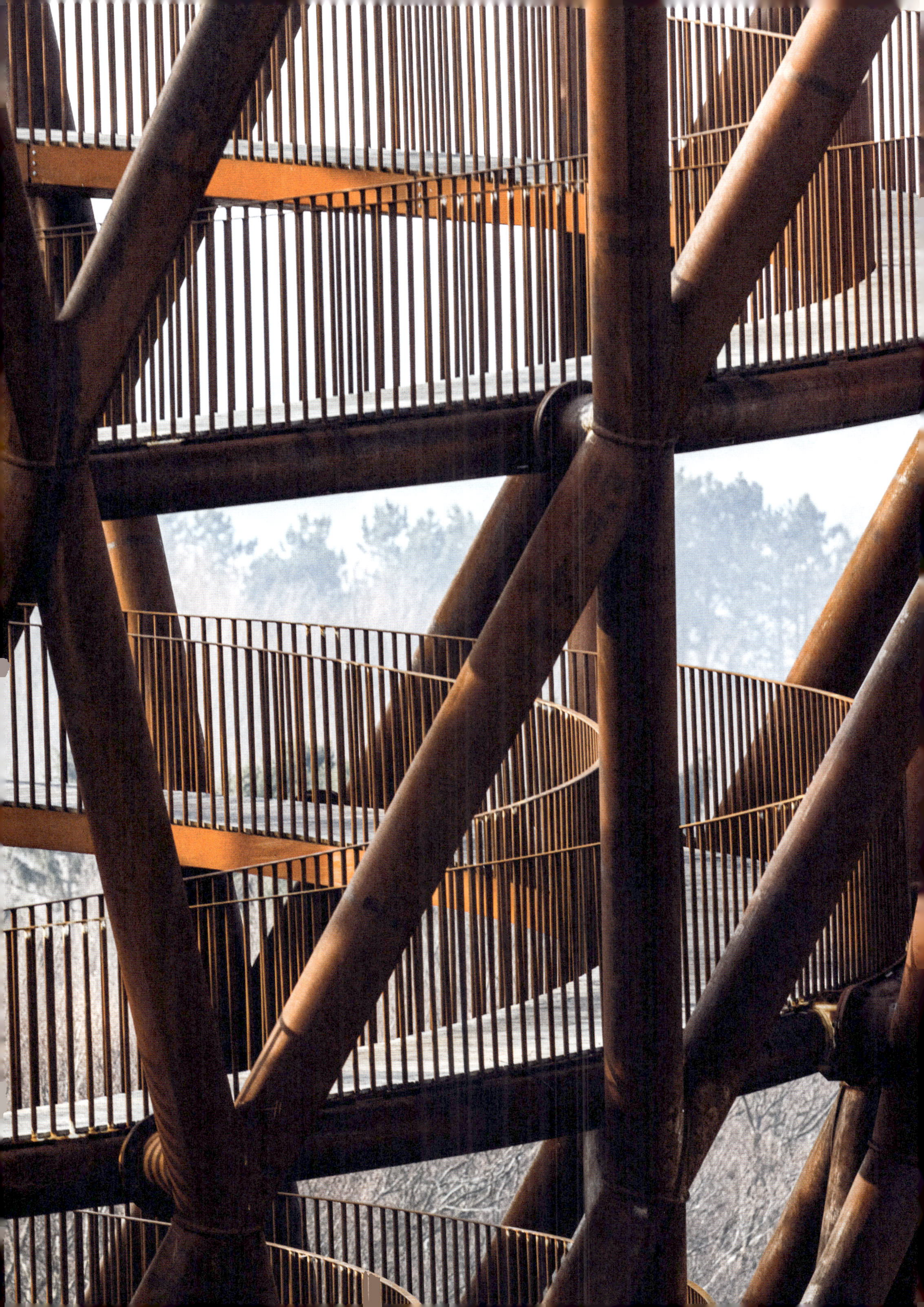

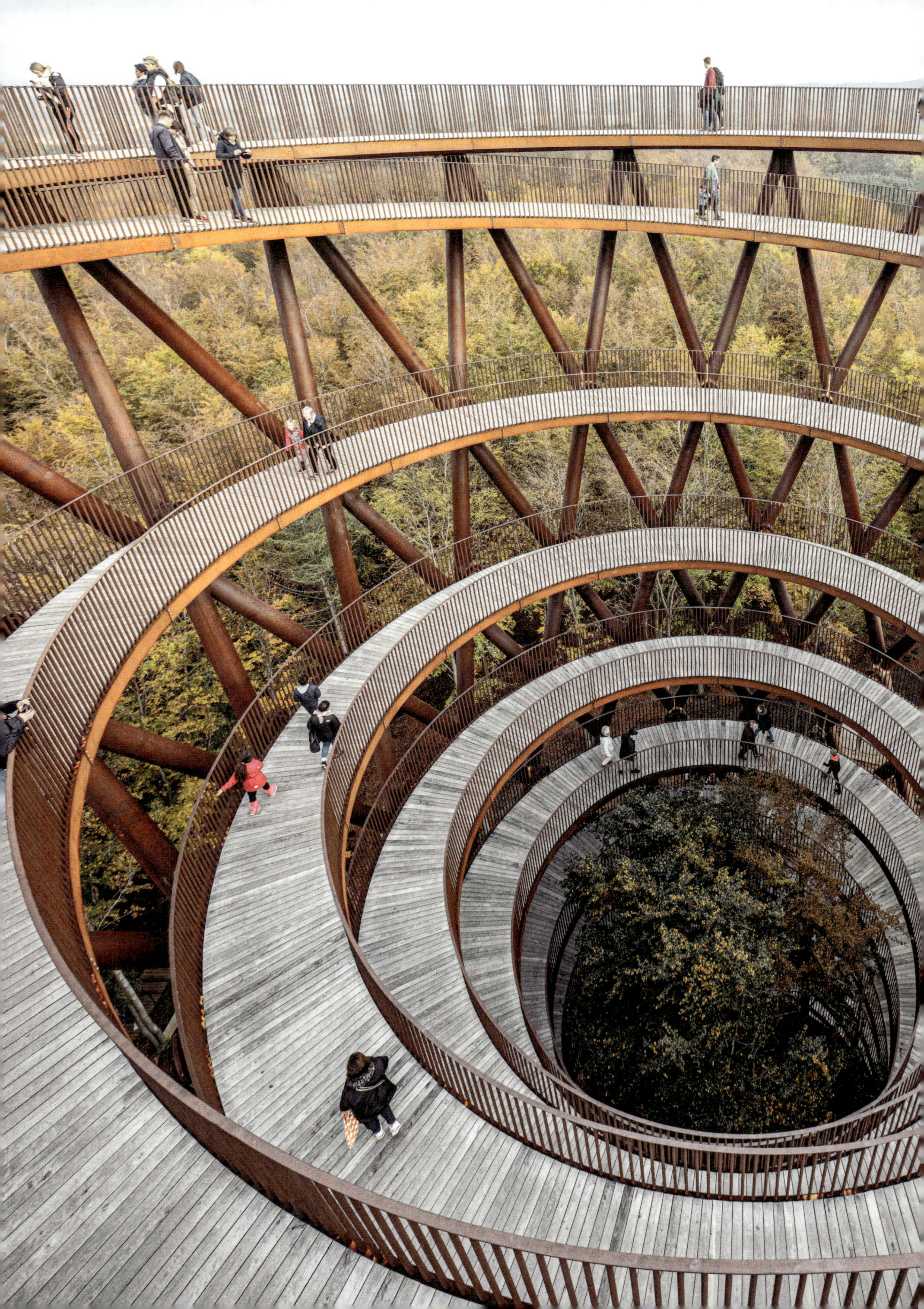

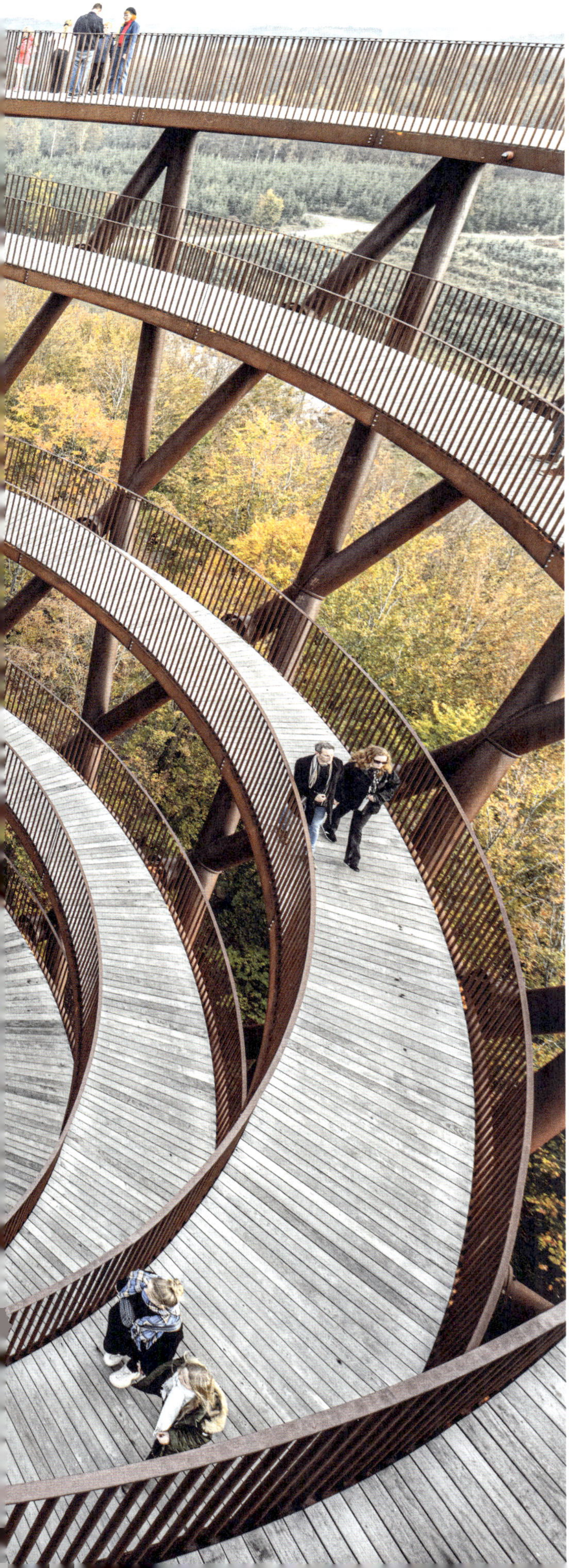

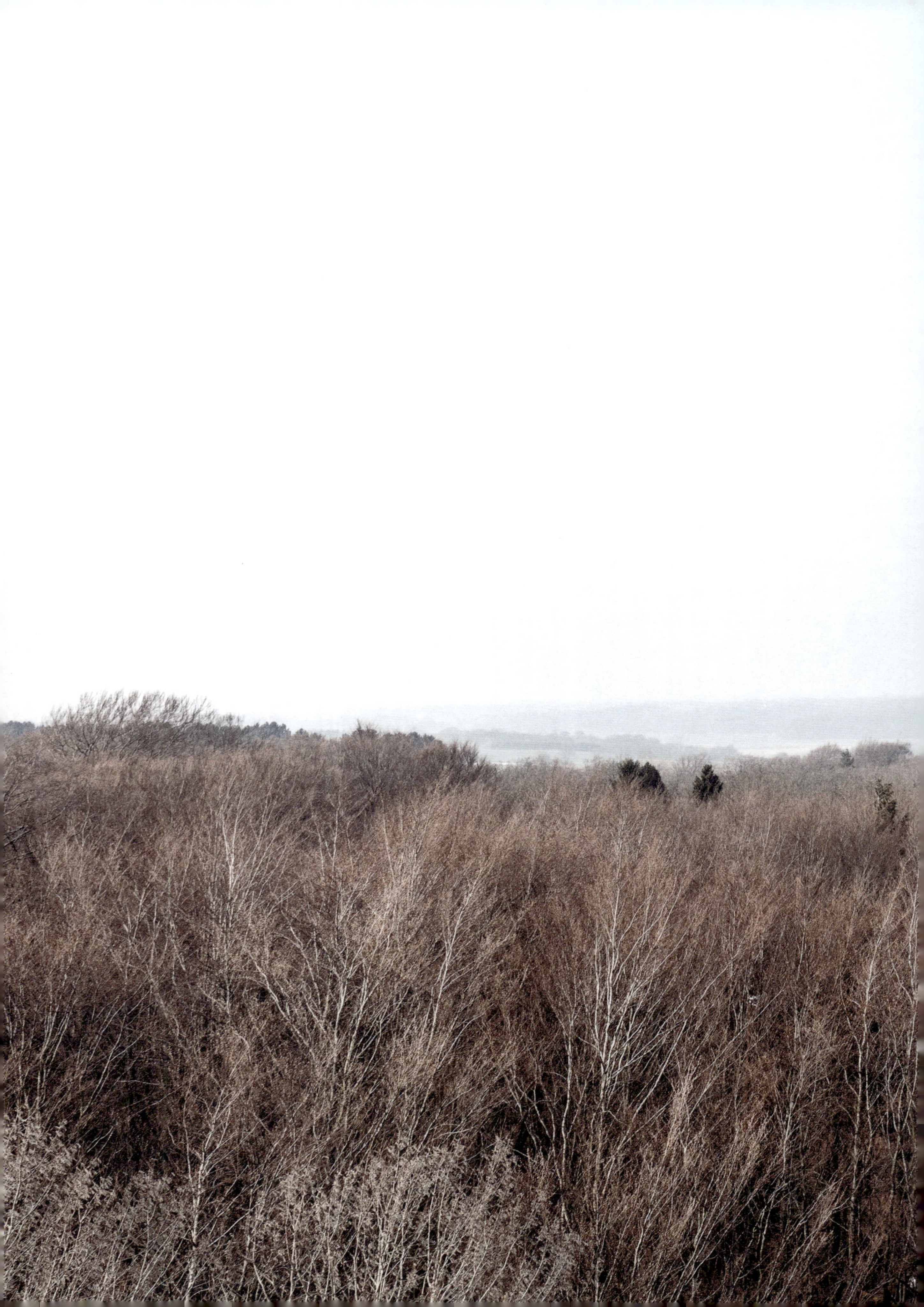

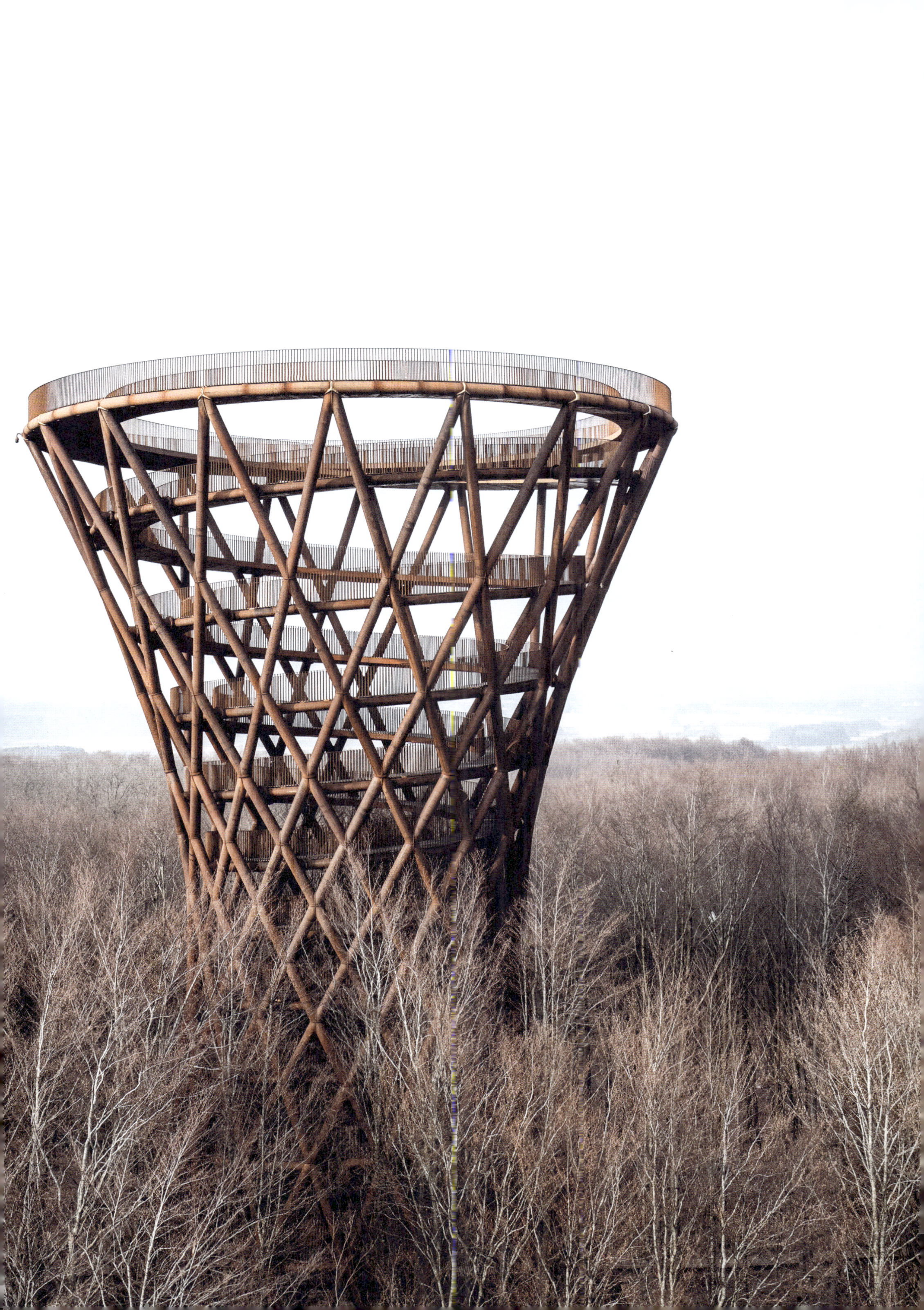

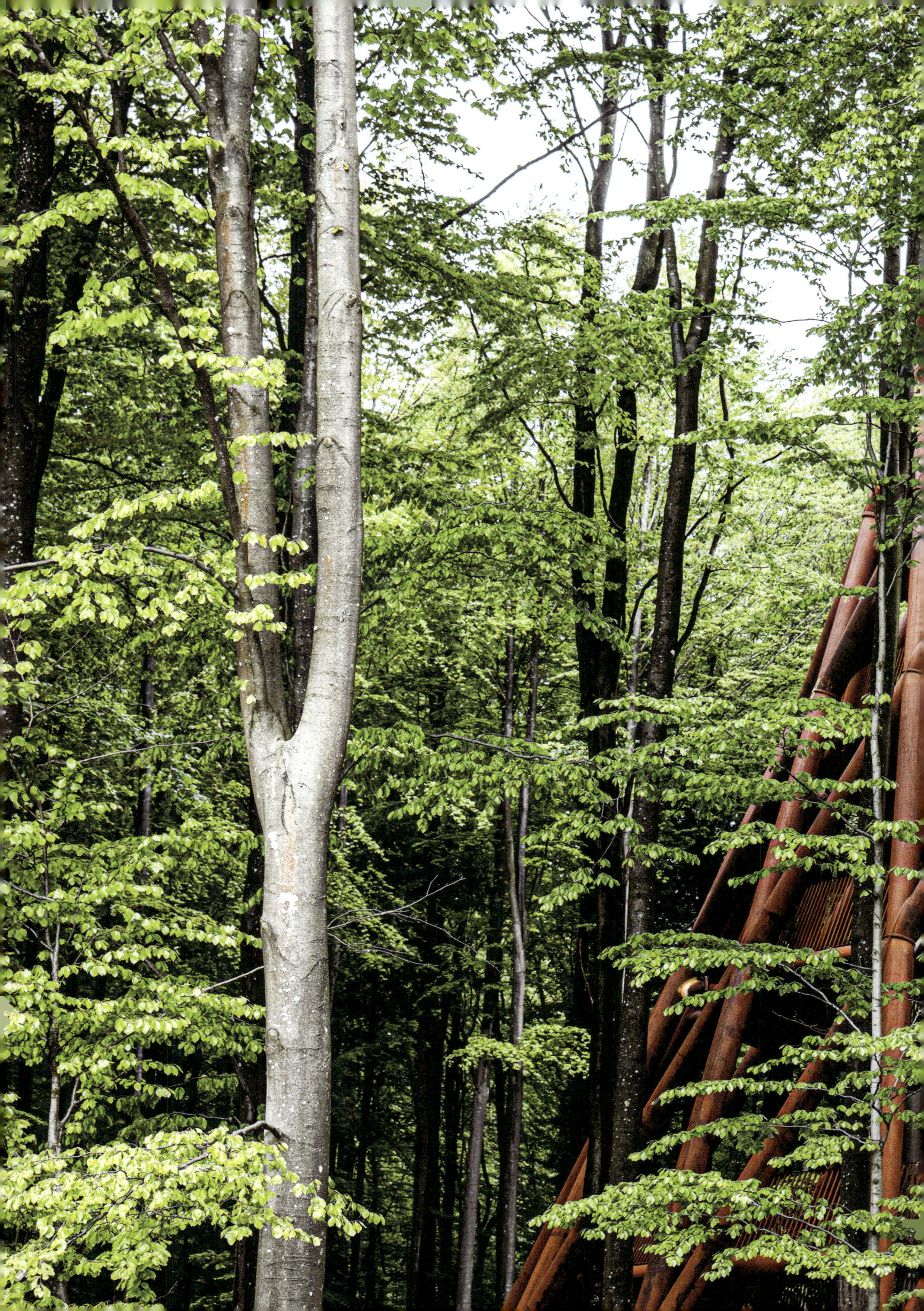

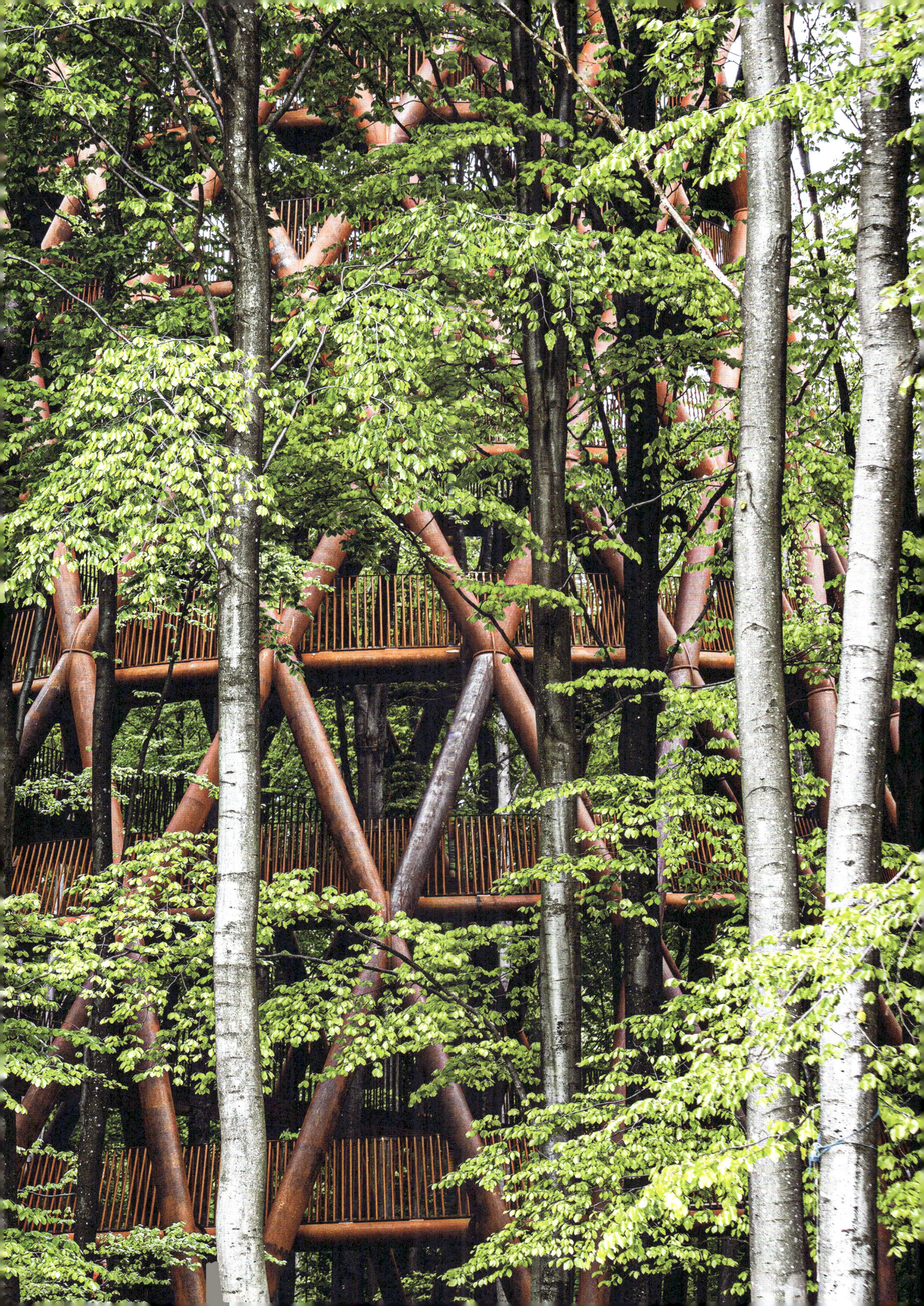

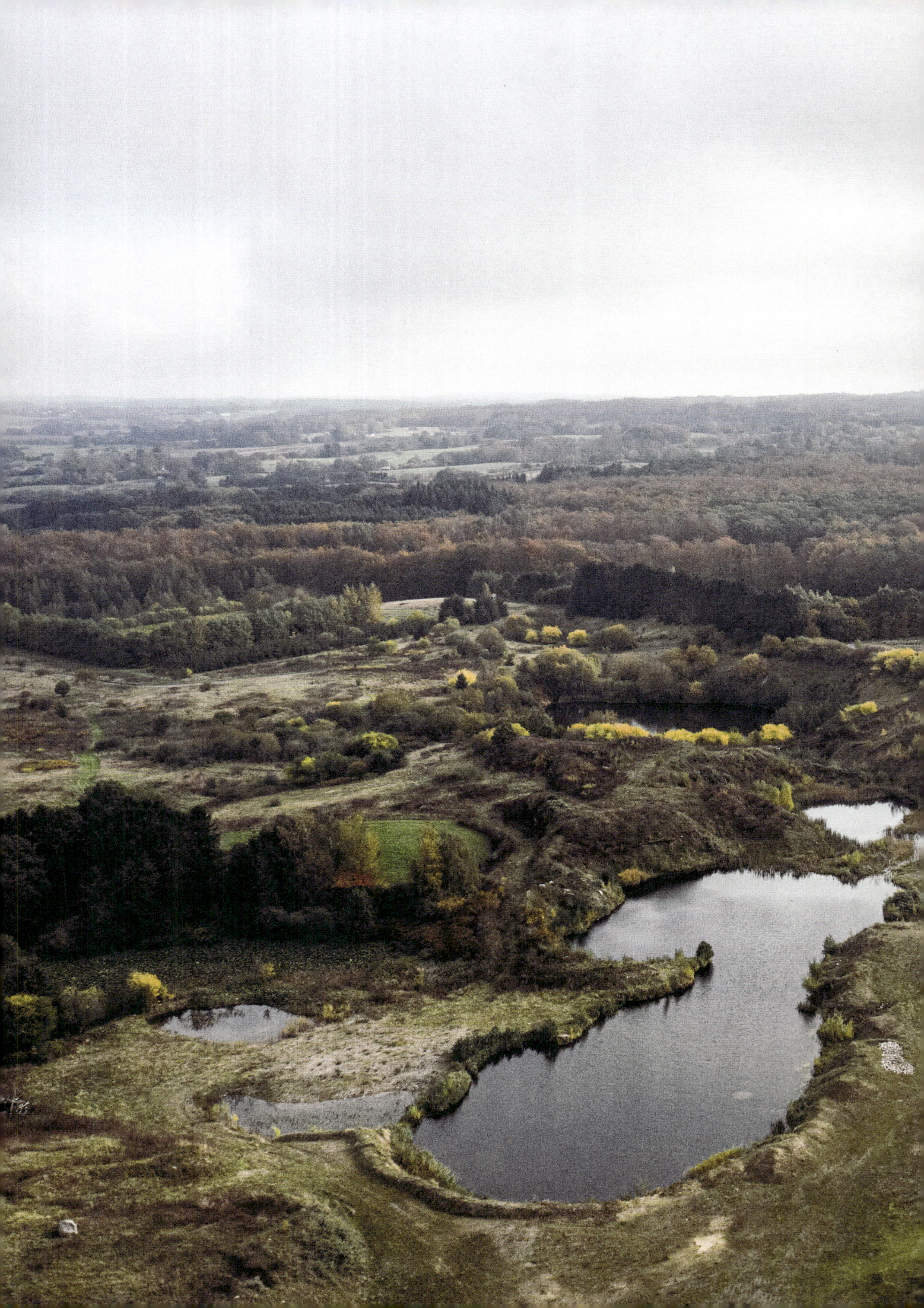

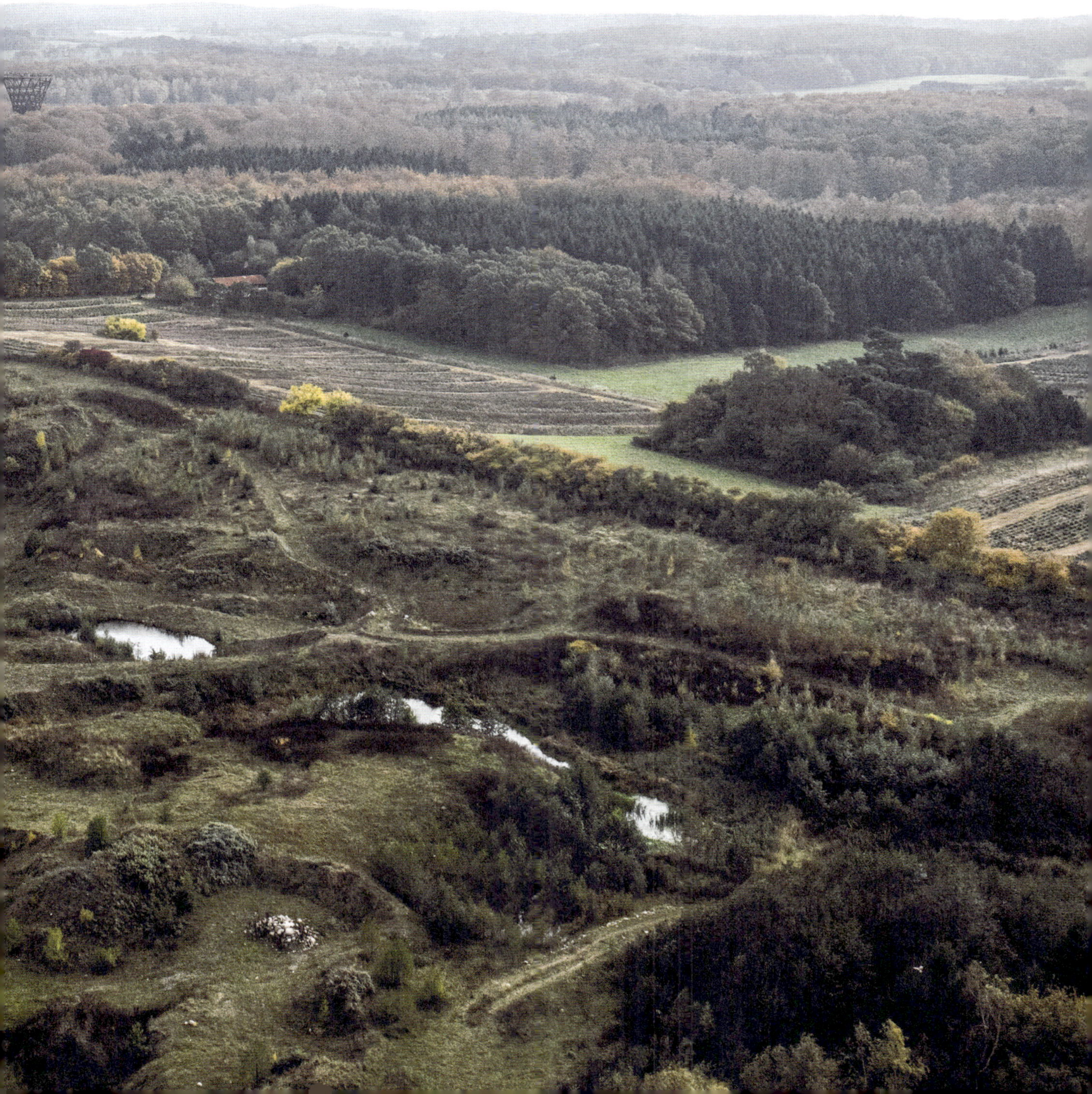

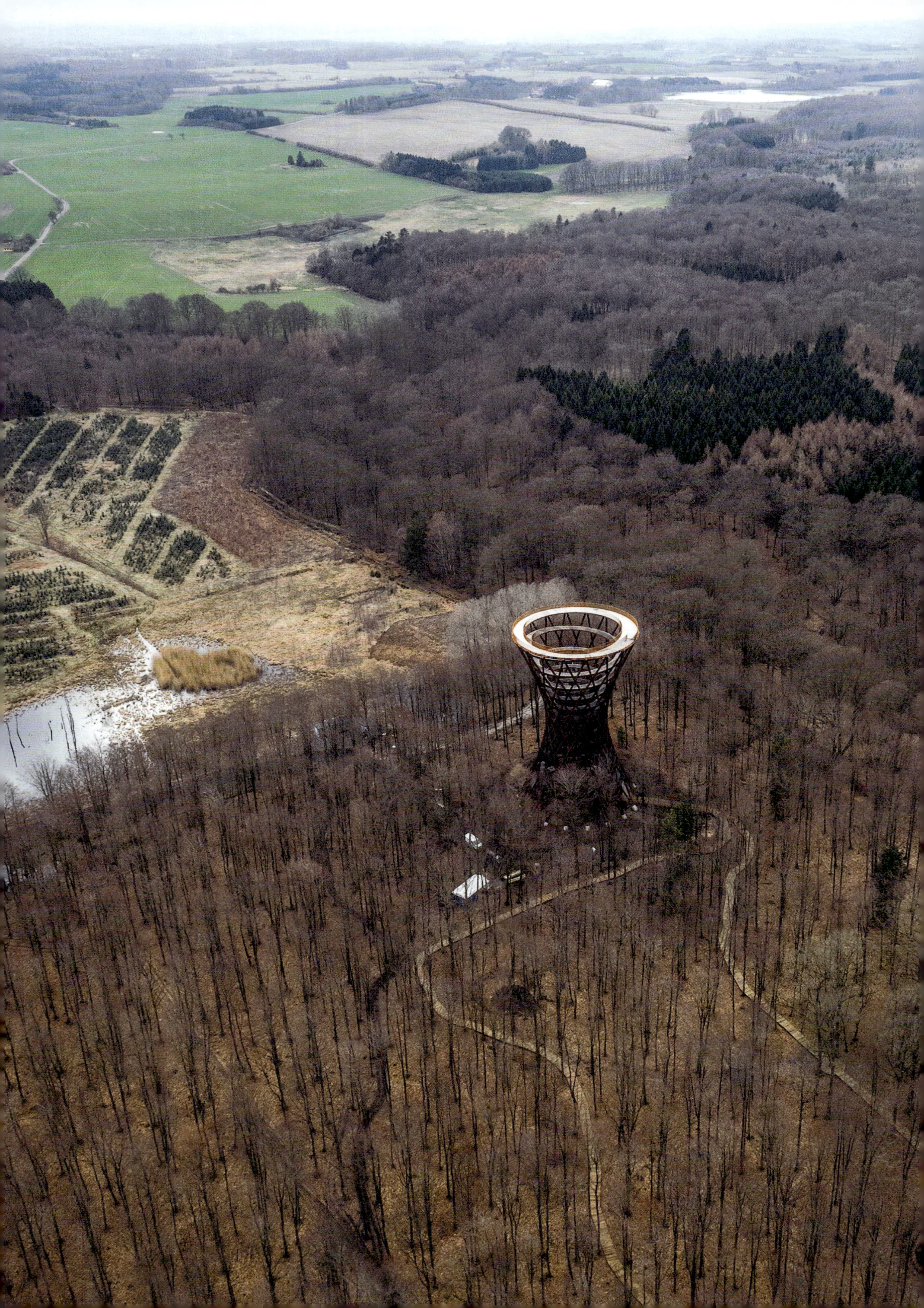

The Forest Tower

Edited by
Kristoffer Lindhardt Weiss

Photos
Rasmus Hjortshøj

Graphic design
Studio Atlant

Translation
Dorte Herholdt Silver

Proofreading
Cornelius Holck Colding

Print
Narayana Press, Denmark, 2020

ISBN 978-87-7407-441-0

Published by
The Danish Architectural Press

Image Credits

Rasmus Hjortshøj: pages 1, 2, 6–15, 17–30, 33–34, 37–38, 40, 42–48, 55–57, 60–61, 64–66, 72–73, 78–79, 82–103, 104
Lars Bjørnsten: page 32
Toni Rubio Soler: page 35
EFFEKT Architects: pages 49–50, 58–59, 62–63, 68, 70–71, 75–76, 81
Camp Adventure: pages 51–54
ICONIC Awards: page 52
Peter Kjeldsen: page 54
Sille Sterll: page 54